...lock
, Jadelrydd Derek Butler
Director/Cyfarwyddwr Terry Hands

ASSOCIATES/AELODAU CYSWLLT

Simon Armstrong	Bradley Freegard	Steven Meo	Robert Perkins
Robert Blythe	Sara Harris-Davies	Dyfrig Morris	Victoria Pugh
Philip Bretherton	Daniel Hawksford	Siwan Morris	Steffan Rhodri
Alun ap Brinley	Lynn Hunter	Simon Nehan	Catrin Rhys
John Cording	Julian Lewis Jones	Kai Owen	Oliver Ryan
Ifan Huw Dafydd	Gwyn Vaughan Jones	Vivien Parry	Owen Teale
Manon Eames	Jenny Livsey	Christian Patterson	Johnson Willis

DIRECTORS/ CYFARWYDDWYR

Tim Baker

Terry Hands

William James

Peter Rowe

DESIGNERS/ CYNLLUNWYR

Mark Bailey

Martyn Bainbridge

Nick Beadle

Timothy O'Brien

COMPOSERS/ CYFANSODDWYR

Dyfan Jones

Colin Towns

ESTHER RUTH ELLIOTT

Esther trained at Bristol Old Vic Theatre School.

Theatre includes: **Once We Were Mothers** (Orange Tree, Richmond), **How to Disappear Completely and Never Be Found** (Sheffield Cruicible), **Intimate Exchanges** (Theatre Royal, Bury St Edmunds), **Three Sisters, Twelfth Night, Pericles** (Shakespeare at the Tobacco Factory), **The Taming of the Shrew, Measure for Measure, Cymbeline** (RSC), **As You Like It** (Arundel Festival), **Killer Joe** (Bristol Old Vic).

Television includes: **Emmerdale, Heartbeat** (YTV), **Casualty** (BBC), **Creature Comforts**.

Radio includes: **Dixon of Dock Green, Evelina, Richard III** (BBC Radio 4).

BETTRYS JONES

Bettrys trained at the Poor School.

Theatre includes: **Box** (Birmingham Rep), **To Kill a Mockingbird** (West Yorkshire Playhouse, Birmingham Rep and on tour), **A Midsummer Night's Dream, The Comedy of Errors** (RSC), **The Little Years** (Orange Tree), **Wait Until Dark** (Garrick), **Party Time/One for the Road** (BAC).

RACHEL LUMBERG

Rachel trained at the Guildhall School of Music and Drama.

Rachel's theatre credits include: **Chatsky** (Almeida Theatre), **Peace in Our Time** (British number one tour), **Katherine Howard** (Chichester Festival Theatre), Victoria Wood's **Talent** (Colchester Theatre), Alan Ayckbourn's **Between Mouthfuls** (Colchester Theatre), **See How They Run** (Salisbury Playhouse), **Woyzeck** (Gate Theatre, London and St Ann's Warehouse, New York), **Il Turco in Italia** (Royal Opera House), **Le nozze di Figaro** (Royal Opera House), **Mog** (Soho Theatre), **Girlfriend Experience** (Royal Court).

Television credits include: **Undercover Heart, The Moonstone, Tears Before Bedtime, Sunburn, Holby City, Hetty Wainthropp, Accused, A Lump in My Throat, Casualty** (BBC), **A Touch of Frost** (ITV) and **A Dance to the Music of Time** (Channel 4).

Feature films include: **Emma** (Matchmaker Films), **South Kensington** (Medusa Films), **Get Me to the Crematorium** (Leda Serene Films).

Radio: **Henry IV part 1** (BBC Radio 4).

SOPHIE STANTON

Writer

Sophie Stanton trained at RADA and has worked extensively as an actor in theatre, film, television and radio since 1991.

Cariad is her first full-length play. It was produced in November 2005 at the Tristan Bates Theatre, London, and awarded her a place in the BBC/Royal Court "50 most promising writers" initiative.

Sophie has been commissioned by the BBC and Channel 4, and is currently under commission by the Bush Theatre, for her second play, **Where Corals Lie**.

PHILLIP BREEN

Director

Phill is Director of New Writing at Clwyd Theatr Cymru.

Productions for CTC: **Two Princes**, **Suddenly Last Summer** and **The Birthday Party**. Other credits include **The Shadow of a Gunman** (Glasgow Citizens), **The Zam Zam Room: an Evening With His Royal Hipness Lord Buckley** (Soho Theatre, Ronnie Scott's and Off-Broadway Time Out New York 'Pick of 2005'), **The Resistible Rise of Arturo Ui** (Glasgow Citizens), **The Promise** (Union Theatre, London), **Far Too Happy** (Edinburgh Fringe and national tour, 2001 Perrier Award

nomination), **A Few Idiots Who Spoil It for Everyone Else** by Tim Key and Mark Watson (Canal Café Theatre, London), **Memoirs of a Dead Man** (Edinburgh Fringe), **Destiny** (BAC, runner up for 2003 James Menzies Kitchen Award). Phillip was director of EDGE04, the Chichester Festival Theatre's Fringe Event, where he directed his adaptation of Bulgakov's **Black Snow** and the BBC rehearsed reading of John Hegley's radio play **The Cat in the Kennel**. Phillip was the curator of the RSC's Laugh-In event which contained original material from Armando Iannucci, Ken Dodd, Alan Plater, Richard Herring, Oliver and Zaltzman, Alex Horne, Mark Watson, and the Cowards. His first play, **Past Imperfect**, was shortlisted for Write2002, the Manchester Royal Exchange's New Writing Award. He co-authored **Director's Shakespeare** to be published by Routledge in March 08.

MARTYN BAINBRIDGE

Designer

Martyn Bainbridge is an Associate of Clwyd Theatr Cymru.

Martyn's productions for Terry Hands at Clwyd Theatr Cymru are: **Memory**, **Arcadia**, **The Crucible**, **Under Milk Wood**, **Night Must Fall**, **The Norman Conquests: Table Manners**, **Living Together**, **Round and Round the Garden**.

Also for CTC: **A Toy Epic**, **Gaslight**, **A Christmas Carol**, **An Inspector Calls** and **The Birthday Party**. Martyn recently designed **A Midsummer Night's Dream** for an Open Air production in Singapore, and **Memory** played Off-Broadway.

Other theatre designs include **Brief Encounter** (West End), and for Theatre Royal Plymouth productions of **A Little Night Music**, **The Birthday Party**, **Kes**, **Absurd Person Singular**, **Charley's Aunt**, **Master Forger**, **I Have Been Here Before**, **Pump Boys and Dinettes**, **The Shadow of a Gunman**.

Designs for other theatre companies include **Measure for Measure** (Nye Teater Oslo), **Deathtrap**, **Intimate Exchanges** (Northcott Theatre), **The Soldier's Tale** (Oxford Playhouse), **On the Razzle** (Leeds Playhouse).

Opera designs include most recently **Don Giovanni** (Royal Scottish Academy), **Ariadne Auf Naxos** (Garsington Opera), **The Magic Flute** (Kent Opera), **The Trial** (Bloomsbury Theatre), **Madame Butterfly** (Phoenix Opera), **Norma**, **La traviata** (Northern Ireland Opera), **Le nozze di Figaro** (Guildhall), **La Rondine** (Royal Academy of Music).

Martyn Bainbridge's ballet designs include **Daphnis and Chloë** (Royal Ballet at Covent Garden).

He has also designed exhibitions and these include **The Astronomers** (London Planetarium), **Armada 1588 – 1988** (National Maritime Museum, Greenwich), **Lawrence of Arabia** (National Portrait Gallery), **Daendels** (Rijksmuseum, Amsterdam), **Madame Tussaud Scenerama**, Amsterdam (entire exhibition) and **The Chamber of Horrors** (Madame Tussaud's, London).

GARETH HUGHES

Lighting Designer

After graduating in computer systems engineering from the University of Wales and working for a short time as an electronics engineer, Gareth began his professional theatre career in 1993 at Clwyd Theatr Cymru, moving from here to the North Wales Theatre in Llandudno, followed by two seasons at Glyndebourne Opera House, before becoming chief electrician at Cambridge Arts Theatre.

In 1999, Gareth began working as a freelance production electrician and lighting programmer for theatre, television and corporate events. Over the next seven years he worked in a wide variety of areas within the entertainment business (from the Royal Shakespeare Company to large corporate events, from major opera festivals to Welsh-language television). During this time he had the opportunity of working alongside some of this country's most respected lighting designers, and on many occasions was responsible for recreating their work on touring productions.

In the summer of 2006 Gareth returned to Clwyd Theatr Cymru as a member of the electrics department.

As well as his extensive production electrics work, Gareth has also worked as a lighting designer, mainly but not exclusively within the world of opera, on a variety of productions ranging from **Educating Rita** (for New Palace Theatre Company) to the UK première of the opera **Hunyadi Laszlo** (for Dorset Opera). Gareth is a professional member of the Association of Lighting Designers.

KEVIN HEYES

Sound Designer

Came to Clwyd Theatr Cymru in 1984 from Leeds Playhouse to join the lighting and sound department. He has been designing lighting and sound for shows ever since, in the Anthony Hopkins Theatre and the Emlyn Williams Theatre, as well as theatres throughout Wales and in Europe. He also teaches lighting and sound design at Scarborough University College and in various colleges around Wales. He redesigned the sound systems in the Anthony Hopkins Theatre and the Emlyn Williams Theatre, with the latest state of the art sound equipment using full digital systems. A big part of his life is now designing firework displays all over Wales and the north-west.

Some of his lighting designs include **The Way It Was, Flora's War, The Secret, The Ballad of Megan Morgan, Mrs Warren's Profession, Our Country's Good, The Daughter-in-Law, Silas Marner, Misalliance** and **My Sister in This House**.

He has now turned his attention full time to sound and all that goes with it. Credits include: **Godspell, Gulliver's Travels, Swallows and Amazons, The Snow Queen, Rape of the Fair Country, A Christmas Carol, The Norman Conquests** trilogy, **Aladdin, Flora's War, Song of the Earth, Dick Whittington, Hard Times, Cinderella - the Panto With Soul, King Lear, Bedroom Farce, The Rabbit, Jack and the Beanstalk, Rosencrantz and Guildenstern Are Dead, The Four Seasons, Robin Hood and the Babes in the Wood, Oh, What a Lovely War!, The Ballad of Megan Morgan, Aladdin - the Red Hot Wok 'n' Roll Panto, One Flew Over the Cuckoo's Nest, Hay Fever, The Mabinogion, Brassed Off, Sleeping Beauty - the Rock 'n' Roll Panto , Troilus and Cressida, A Streetcar Named Desire, Sugar, The Way It Was, Dick Whittington - the Rock'n' Roll Panto, Present Laughter, An Inspector Calls, Beauty and the Beast, Of Mice and Men, Suddenly Last Summer, A Toy Epic** and **Jack and the Beanstalk**.

DANIEL LLEWELYN-WILLIAMS

Fight Director

Daniel is a native South Walian and trained at LAMDA.

Theatre credits include: **Suddenly Last Summer**, **An Inspector Calls**, **Troilus and Cressida**, **Brassed Off** (Clwyd Theatr Cymru); **Romans in Britain**, (Sheffield Crucible); **The Three Musketeers** (Titchfield Abbey Festival), **My Sainted Aunt** (the New End Theatre), **Macbeth**, **A Midsummer Night's Dream** (Tour de Force).

Film credits include: **Vanity Fair** (Focus Features); **Charlotte Grey** (Warner Bros); **The Gigolos** (Punk Productions); **Down in the Tube Station at Midnight** (Big Boy Productions).

Television credits include: **EastEnders** (BBC), **Torchwood** (BBC), **Ultimate Force II** (Bentley Productions), **The Birthday Show** (Helter Skelter).

At LAMDA: **On the Town**; **Scenes From the New World**; **Hobson's Choice**; **Today** by Robert Holman; **The Innocent Mistress**; **Romeo and Juliet**; **Mother Clap**; **Coriolanus**.

Daniel's Fight Directing credits include: **Two Princes** (Clwyd Theatr Cymru), **The Three Musketeers** (Titchfield Abbey); **Hamlet** (Wild Thyme); **The Things We Do For Love**, **Private Lives**, **The Romans in Britain**.

Daniel assisted Terry King in choreographing **Troilus and Cressida** for Terry Hands at Clwyd Theatr Cymru. Daniel also twice won the coveted first prize at LAMDA's Fight Night.

CARIAD

Sophie Stanton

cariad / (*noun*) love, beloved one, darling

for 'yer mother' . . .

Do you want the moon to play with
Or the stars to run away with?
They'll come if you don't cry

Cariad was first performed at the Tristan Bates Theatre, London, on 23 November 2005 with the following cast:

BLODWEN   Sophie Stanton
JAYNE   Rachel Sanders
EMILY   Becky John

Director   Ken Christiansen
Designer   Robin Don
Lighting Designer   Prema Mehta

Author's Acknowledgements

I'd like to thank Ken Christiansen, Bernadette Davis, Robin Don, Guy Jenkins, Suli Majithia, Lucy Morrison, Willy Russell, the Actors Centre and Clwyd Theatr Cymru for their exceptional constancy, enthusiasm and support.

I should also like to acknowledge the extraordinary memory of 'yer father', Cedric. With infinite gratitude and respect.

Your absence is a great presence.

Cariad,
you twats from hell!

Characters

BLODWEN, *mid-thirties*
JAYNE, *mid-thirties*
EMILY, *nine*

A forward slash in the text (/) marks the point at which the next speaker interrupts.

This text went to press before the end of rehearsals and so may differ slightly from the play as performed.

ACT ONE

Scene One

*The living room of a chaotic two-up two-down, mid-Wales.
Night. Rain. At one end, the front door and staircase. At the
other, a door leading to the kitchen off. A sofa, an armchair, a
Welsh dresser, a coffee table, a grandmother clock – each
piece from a separate decade – and detritus from generations
past; the random accumulation of lives lived and left.
Moments pass. Car headlights appear across the window, an
engine is turned off.*

A key is heard in the lock and the door opens. BLODWEN
*enters – wild hair, an oddball. Somehow, she makes total sense
of the room.*

BLODWEN. I'm mad, me. In you come, love.

The door swings shut behind her.

BLODWEN *is under the impression that* JAYNE *has
followed her into the house, but the door has slammed shut
in her face.*

BLODWEN *turns on three separate side lights.*

D'you know this morning, right? I'm getting up. I put on my
daughter's dressing gown! Don't know what I'm bloody
doing, right. Comes up to y'here on me, look. Don't even
bloody notice. I'll shed some light on the situation.

BLODWEN *sees that* JAYNE *is not in the room. She goes to
the stairs and shouts up.*

Bog's up the top, if you need it. Lid's up. I like your coat. I
bet that got on his tits, did it?

BLODWEN *turns on a two-bar electric fire.*

Walks round the house for three hours like a rug rat. Not my fault. Nobody bloody tells you, do they? Allun goes out to work without a look.

BLODWEN *shifts piles of washing, newspapers, etc. from the sofa to the floor.*

Cwtch up and mind that. There's springs sticking out like pigs' arses.

There's a knock at the front door.

What now? I'll put the fire's going on.

BLODWEN *goes out to the kitchen. We hear the sound of a kettle being filled and switched on.*

(*Offstage.*) Will I tell you a funny story, right? You will die!

BLODWEN *comes out of the kitchen.*

What did I come in the room for?

BLODWEN *starts at something.*

Oh! Look at me, I'm still in my coat! Mad. Right. I'll put the kettle's going on.

BLODWEN *goes out to the kitchen. There's another knock at the door.*

(*Offstage.*) I were going up the Tick, right. The other day. What're we having, tea? Bring you round from your day this time of night. Right. So. I'm going up by there, I can't remember what for now. But. So. No. See. So. I bumped into Mary my friend. Oh love her, it's a shame. I think she might be rotting. You have to feel sorry on it, don't you though? She goes, 'You want to get yourself up round Dod the Meat's on offer!' She is good. I went mad in there, I could feed a five hundred. Lady Luck look, having you to stay.

BLODWEN *comes out of the kitchen.*

What was it I were meant to be doing? Coat! I'd forget my head if it weren't switched on. Right.

BLODWEN *goes out. Another knock at the door. The letter box opens and* JAYNE *speaks through it.*

JAYNE (*offstage*). Hello?

BLODWEN (*offstage*). Hello!

JAYNE (*offstage*). Hello.

The letter box closes.

BLODWEN (*offstage*). What're you doing there?

Pause. The letter box opens.

JAYNE (*offstage*). Should I come back later?

BLODWEN (*offstage*). What for?

JAYNE (*offstage*). It's inconvenient, is it?

BLODWEN (*offstage*). Is it?

JAYNE (*offstage*). I didn't mean to put you out. I did say.

The letter box closes.

BLODWEN (*offstage*). I know! Are we having a game, we are?

The following speech marks denote the game BLODWEN *thinks they are playing:*

'Do come in!' Put you out . . . Don't her talk marvellous. I'm not enough to keep up. Let me think, let me think on it. Oh right, I have a good one. You'll love this, you – 'I'll get the girl to bring us our tea. She's only fastened to the mangle!'

The letter box opens.

JAYNE. (*offstage*) Sorry.

BLODWEN (*offstage*). S'alright!

JAYNE (*offstage*). I'll – I'll come back . . .

BLODWEN (*offstage*). 'Do! Anytime.'

The letter box closes.

(*Claps*.) I'm having it! Make yourself at home, look. 'Doos what you want and gets what you're given round y'here.'

The letter box opens.

Right? Am I having you for supper?

JAYNE (*offstage*). Are you talking to me?

BLODWEN (*offstage*). No, I'm talking to the cat. If I'd knowed I were getting a visit, I'd of swept.

The letter box closes. And opens.

JAYNE (*offstage*). Is there a telephone?

BLODWEN (*offstage*). I've not had this much fun since Glyn choked on his Christmas. Just when you think it's a world of wet echo comes the sun to the hill. Duw Anwyl.

JAYNE (*offstage*). Can I use your phone?

BLODWEN (*offstage*). I've no phone, see.

JAYNE (*offstage*). My battery's died. I might just going to have to walk and try and walk back to the pub.

BLODWEN (*offstage*). 'Cheese and onion if you're going, and an ickle pickled egg.'

JAYNE (*offstage*). It's raining, you see.

BLODWEN (*offstage*). Old ladies and their sticks!

JAYNE (*offstage*). Cats and dogs.

BLODWEN (*offstage*). Not from round y'here are you, 'cos I'm good with faces, see? Don't her talk nice. In my lovely cowing shit pit, you're alright to stay?

JAYNE (*offstage*). I've definitely missed the train?

BLODWEN (*offstage*). I know.

JAYNE (*offstage*). Maybe I should try and find the man?

BLODWEN (*offstage*). Spitty Del?

JAYNE (*offstage*). I didn't like him.

BLODWEN (*offstage*). He fancied his chances with you!

D'you take sugar?

Pause.

Lady? (*Beat.*) 'Lady Ladybird?' (*Beat.*) Do you take sugar?

BLODWEN *comes out of the kitchen.*

I just made that up, look. 'Fly away home!'

The letter box opens.

JAYNE (*offstage*). I do need somewhere now, you see.

BLODWEN. 'You've come to the right place!' What's she doing there?

BLODWEN *goes to the door, bends down, talks through the letter box.*

'Hello.'

JAYNE (*offstage*). Oh God! You made me jump!

BLODWEN. What're you doing there?

JAYNE (*offstage*). Door shut.

BLODWEN. What's the door doing shut?

JAYNE (*offstage*). I thought you had somebody in there.

BLODWEN. So did I, so I did!

JAYNE (*offstage*). Who?

BLODWEN. You! You'll catch your bloody death there, girl.

The letter box closes. BLODWEN *knocks from the inside. The letter box opens.*

'Can I come in?'

JAYNE (*offstage*). No – Can I come in?

BLODWEN. 'No!'

JAYNE (*offstage*). I'm not meant to be here.

BLODWEN. You are not meant to be there! I've got the kettle's on. Snug up.

BLODWEN *starts to walk back to the kitchen*. JAYNE *knocks on the letter box*. BLODWEN *goes to the front door, opens it*.

'Hello!'

JAYNE (*offstage*). What are you doing?

BLODWEN. What are you doing? You daft.

BLODWEN *comes in leaving the door ajar, goes back to kitchen*. JAYNE *overbalances, falls into the room. She struggles to her feet – immaculately dressed and groomed, hair shines, skin glows . . . She carries a large expensive leather bag. She is clearly very drunk.*

(*Offstage*.) Fuck off, you cow!

JAYNE. Oh God!

BLODWEN *comes out of the kitchen*.

BLODWEN. Do you take sugar?

JAYNE. No.

BLODWEN. You never! Where do you put it? D'you want some stew I baked yesterday? You can have Allun's, he don't deserve it. Right, I've decided. It's going on, 'cos I'm having some.

JAYNE. I don't eat meat.

BLODWEN. Don't worry, I'll pick it out. That cat's a pig! I goes in the kitchen, right. She's stood on top of the stove helping itself from the pot. If there's any hairs take them out.

BLODWEN *goes into the kitchen*.

JAYNE. Don't. I feel a bit . . . Don't worry.

BLODWEN (*offstage*). It's no trouble. Sog up your juices. You been there long, like?

JAYNE. Where?

BLODWEN (*offstage*). The Pickles.

JAYNE. The pub?

BLODWEN (*offstage*). You was out of your pod!

JAYNE. I don't drink!

BLODWEN (*offstage*). You do! Did you mind him being like that with you though? He's been a miserable cow since his horse got shot. You can force a shit on strangers.

BLODWEN *comes out of the kitchen.*

Did he spit?

JAYNE. Yes!

BLODWEN. Thought so.

JAYNE. I shouldn't have talked to him . . . I sort of thought I recognised him. I sort of thought –

BLODWEN. I heard that said before, but it's just that he looks like a stamp.

BLODWEN *goes out to the kitchen.* JAYNE *goes to sit in the armchair.*

'I've a strange visitor.'

JAYNE. Who?

BLODWEN (*offstage*). 'You!' I'll chop you into liver if you don't give it up, girl!

JAYNE *sits heavily into the armchair, it tips over backwards.* BLODWEN *comes out of the kitchen and appears not to notice, as* JAYNE *struggles to right herself.*

I never normally go up there myself. I only popped by on my way back from the station. You're not on your holiday, are you?

JAYNE. No! No.

BLODWEN. No. I knew that, I'm like that, me. What're you doing round y'here then?

JAYNE. I should've found a hotel.

BLODWEN. No, love. Most glamourous we have round y'here is the clock. What's your name, Ladybird? 'Ladybird, fly away home, your house is on fire, your children are gone'?

JAYNE. Pardon?

BLODWEN. I don't even know its name, 'my strange visitor'!

JAYNE. Jayne.

Beat.

BLODWEN. Where?

JAYNE. Here. Sorry. What? Me.

BLODWEN. What?

JAYNE. I'm Jayne. Sorry.

BLODWEN. No!

JAYNE. Yes.

BLODWEN. Jayne!

JAYNE. What?

BLODWEN. I don't believe you. Is it?

JAYNE. Yes!

BLODWEN. My favourite name, Jayne. Duw, there's beauty for you.

BLODWEN *goes back to kitchen.*

Jayne!

JAYNE. What?

BLODWEN (*offstage*). Duw.

JAYNE. God.

BLODWEN (*offstage*). 'Jayne has come to stay!'

JAYNE. Look. I don't want to put you out.

BLODWEN (*offstage*). I'm in, bloody girl! I'm having you with pleasure.

BLODWEN *comes out.*

Will I take your lovely coat?

JAYNE. No.

BLODWEN. You cold? I'll put the fire's going on.

JAYNE. No . . .

BLODWEN. I'm not having it.

BLODWEN *goes to the fire which is already on.*

Who done that?

JAYNE. Sorry?

BLODWEN. S'alright.

A moment. They study one another. BLODWEN *goes back to the kitchen.*

(*Offstage.*) And you was meant to be catching your train home?

JAYNE. I did.

BLODWEN (*offstage*). You never. You missed it.

JAYNE. What?

BLODWEN (*offstage*). When?

JAYNE. I used to live here. / You see.

BLODWEN (*offstage*). You never.

JAYNE. I did. / We moved.

BLODWEN (*offstage*). I'd of known.

JAYNE. Never thought I'd come back, hopefully.

BLODWEN (*offstage*). When? / Did you live here?

JAYNE. Only here for death. I was eight, or something.

A pot smashes in the kitchen. JAYNE jumps. BLODWEN comes out carrying two mugs of tea. She is clearly shaken.

BLODWEN. Oh Christ. Oh Daddy. Where?

JAYNE. What?

BLODWEN. Did you live.

JAYNE. Here.

BLODWEN. No. Where?

JAYNE. Behind the church / – the chapel.

BLODWEN. Behind the chapel – No!

JAYNE. Yes!

BLODWEN. Jayne!

JAYNE. Yes! / – What?

BLODWEN. It's me!

JAYNE. I know! 'Hello!'

Beat.

BLODWEN. Blod! Blod, you bloody daft bloody cow! Blodwen!

JAYNE. Oh God.

BLODWEN. Oh Christ, I don't get over it. Frig-a-doon, I'll have to sit. Frig-a-bloody-doon. I knew it were you. In a moment. I knew it! Come y'here and give me an hug!

BLODWEN goes to JAYNE, arms outstretched. JAYNE takes the tea from BLODWEN. BLODWEN embraces JAYNE.

You could smack my chops with a sack of dirty herons. Why didn't you phone?

JAYNE. Sorry?

BLODWEN. Bloody hero bloody worshipped you, me, and you up and bloody leave me when I'm nine! Why didn't you phone?

JAYNE. Sorry . . .

BLODWEN. Come y'here.

BLODWEN *embraces* JAYNE.

JAYNE. Put these down.

BLODWEN. Give it y'here.

BLODWEN *takes the mugs of tea from* JAYNE.

I don't believe you're here, it's you!

JAYNE. 'It's me!'

BLODWEN. I'm that excited, I'm a muffin.

BLODWEN *embraces* JAYNE.

I had a feeling about today. How's your bum for love bites?

JAYNE. Sorry?

BLODWEN. You married?

JAYNE. No. No.

BLODWEN. Bugger me, it's good to see you now. Got a boyfriend?

JAYNE. No. Actually.

BLODWEN. No, I don't believe you. Only good man's a dead one, innit?

JAYNE. No.

BLODWEN. No. I'm being daft, don't worry. Christ. Beautiful you are, and you're not even courting.

JAYNE. Shush!

BLODWEN. I can't get round it. I can't go over it. I'll have to go through it.

JAYNE. What?

BLODWEN. You wait 'til I tell my sister. She'll be green as a sow. D'you remember Angharad?

JAYNE. No.

BLODWEN. Golden hand and lip of bone? Cowing annoying she is. Sit down, love, I'll not have polite in my house. Not coming out of you! And I've got a daughter.

BLODWEN *goes to the dresser, takes a photo frame.*

That's Emily, look.

BLODWEN *hands photo to* JAYNE.

(*Indicating armchair.*) Don't go nowhere near that thing, mind, it's the cat's bed. She's had babies in that, she has. Loads. She's quite fat, but I'm not worrying about it.

JAYNE. She will be if she's had lots of babies.

BLODWEN. Not the cat, you daft! Emily, I mean. She'll love you! She is a house for nine. Married the first bugger that come along, me, and he's not a kisser, mind.

JAYNE. Oh, well that's good. What's that smell?

BLODWEN. Oh Christ, you're right. It'll burn to turd! Good influence on me, you. See? I used to steal from purses! Put your foot down on that didn't you, with a firm hand? Love her. Right. It's coming out, I can't wait!

BLODWEN *goes to the kitchen. During the following,* JAYNE *goes to her bag, takes out an urn. Places it carefully on the dresser. Takes out a half-empty bottle of whisky. Pours a large dose in her tea. Takes a swig from the bottle. Puts the bottle back in her bag.*

(*Offstage.*) Ten-and-half pound of baby she was, coming out. They was talking about it round y'here for weeks, you missed out on all that. Like shitting a chapel, it's no wonder. I mean, I have to say 'no' to her, like. I goes, 'No, Em. You'll have to wait!' And her face. Cracks me up, it does. She goes,

'Mam? Mam can I have a pizza?' I goes, 'Emily Evans, you have two hopes. Bob Hope and no hope, you've just had your roast cowing chicken dinner with all the trimmings!' (*Beat.*) She might have worms, I expect. I can't wait for her to take up smoking! I forgot your sugar, look!

JAYNE. No no, it's alright.

BLODWEN (*offstage*). You're alright, it's no trouble.

BLODWEN *comes out with a sugar bowl, stirs two spoonfuls into* JAYNE*'s tea.*

D'you want kids?

JAYNE. I'm not sure. Anymore.

BLODWEN. No! Well you have to think of your back!

JAYNE. I don't take sugar.

BLODWEN. I thought you said. Didn't you say? I must be hearing things. You can have mine, look. You can have that.

JAYNE. No! No, / I didn't mean that.

BLODWEN. Polite? House? No!

BLODWEN *swaps over the mugs of tea.*

See, no kids and you're not married. You are brave!

JAYNE. You are!

BLODWEN. Too bloody right I bloody am!

JAYNE. Where are they tonight?

BLODWEN. Who?

JAYNE. Your. Daughter?

BLODWEN. He'll of taken her up my sister's then he'll not have to speak to her, like.

BLODWEN *takes a swig of tea and considers it.*

Milk's off. He's not very good with Em on his own.

JAYNE. I'm dreadful with kids.

BLODWEN. Says they've nothing in common. I don't blame him. She takes after me, it's no fun – You are! You was good to me!

There's a knock at the door.

You know what we've been forgetting?

JAYNE. Are you going to get that?

BLODWEN. It's coming up, hold your horses.

BLODWEN *hands* JAYNE *her tea. They touch wrists and toast.*

Kill you with kindness!

JAYNE. Kill you with kindness!

They each take a sip from their own cups across one another's hands. A moment. They part.

BLODWEN. Oh Christ! That'll put hairs on your tits. D'you have any hairs on your tits?

JAYNE. No.

BLODWEN. I have, me. Loads. Right, it's coming out.

BLODWEN *goes out to the kitchen.* JAYNE *goes to the door, opens the letter box, nobody there. She goes to her bag for the whisky – swigs, pours some in her tea, replaces the bottle.*

(*Offstage.*) Do you remember that headmistress? / Pimps?

JAYNE. No. / Pimps! – Bloody hell.

BLODWEN (*offstage*). And Jenkins the Sigh. They'll all be bloody dead now.

JAYNE. Hopefully.

BLODWEN *comes in from kitchen.*

BLODWEN. D'you remember Mr Wankovski?

JAYNE. No.

BLODWEN. You do! You rescued me when them girls pushed me down the stairs outside his office. You kicked Twiggy in the tits. You don't remember?

JAYNE. I was shy!

BLODWEN. Brilliant, you was. Like an angry bruise. You was bloody May Queen!

JAYNE. Oh! / I was. Was I?

BLODWEN goes out to the kitchen.

BLODWEN (*offstage*). You have to remember that. I was so proud of you that day. My mate. And Pimps turned up in freezer bags on her feet to stop chalk markings going on her best shoes. And I was a fat fairy looking up. Why d'you wear your best shoes and then cover them up in food wrap?

There's a knock at the door.

JAYNE. I'll get it, shall I?

BLODWEN (*offstage*). You always did!

JAYNE goes to answer it. There's nobody there.

JAYNE. Hello?

BLODWEN (*offstage*). 'Hello!'

BLODWEN comes out with two steaming plates piled high with stew.

'Do come in!'

JAYNE. Oh.

BLODWEN. It's you!

JAYNE. Hello.

BLODWEN. Get your chops round this, look. She was a bit of a cow when I think on it.

JAYNE. Who?

BLODWEN. Pimps.

JAYNE. She was a megalomaniacal bloody despot as far as I can remember! And she tortured little boys!

BLODWEN. You haven't changed, have you? Best days of your life, innit? My mother'll die, I can't wait. Sup up! Right then, I'm having that bit. And I'm having that bit. And I'll have that bit there.

BLODWEN *picks chunks of meat off* JAYNE's *plate with a sharp knife and puts it on her own.*

How's your mam, love?

JAYNE. Sorry?

BLODWEN. Always smelling of wood smoke, your mam. And a song for every occasion, love her.

JAYNE. D'you mind if I use your lavatory?

BLODWEN. Top of the stairs, did I say? Lid's up.

JAYNE. Right.

JAYNE *goes out up the stairs.*

BLODWEN. Mad!

> (*Singing.*) Come come come
> Remember you're a plum
> Don't start a-hollering if things look glum
> It doesn't matter what the weather
> Plums will always hang together
> Come come come
> Remember you're a plum.

We hear the sound of JAYNE *peeing upstairs.* BLODWEN *has a sudden realisation – an awful memory floods back.*

Oh, Dad! Oh, Daddy! Oh frig-a-bloody-doon.

BLODWEN *puts down her plate, struggles to her feet. Goes to bottom of the stairs and shouts –*

Jayne!!! Jayne!

JAYNE (*offstage*). Down in a minute.

BLODWEN. Oh Christ, girl. Why didn't you say? Oh my aching arseholes, I don't believe you.

JAYNE (*offstage*). Is everything alright?

BLODWEN. You're alright, love. You'll be right. You're y'here now, I'll see to it. Oh Duw. Duw Anwyl. Tell me no, I'm not having it!

> BLODWEN *sees the urn on the side for the first time. She screams, loud and long.*

JAYNE (*offstage*). Jesus! What's the matter?

BLODWEN. Oh Christ help us, now.

> BLODWEN *picks up a crucifix from the dresser, holds it up to the urn. She still has the knife.*

See you. See. No! See! I had a feeling about today. I'm not having it! You go!

> *We hear* JAYNE *rushing down the stairs. She bursts into the room, tights around her ankles.*

JAYNE. What's the matter?

> *She falls onto the coffee table and lands in the stew.*

BLODWEN. Jayne!

JAYNE. What's the matter?

BLODWEN. What's the matter?

JAYNE. You scared me!

BLODWEN. You scared me!

> BLODWEN *picks up the urn.*

JAYNE. What are you doing?

BLODWEN. You have come to die!

JAYNE. Am I going mad?

BLODWEN. You're alright, love. You're okay.

JAYNE. Am I?

BLODWEN. No.

Silence.

JAYNE. I don't want it.

BLODWEN. I don't want it for you. I'll put it up safe by y'here look. For when you're ready.

BLODWEN *puts the urn on top of the Welsh dresser.*

Pause.

JAYNE. Don't do anything.

Can't even what I came for, up that hill . . . Couldn't even bring myself.

Beat.

BLODWEN. Could you do with your tea?

JAYNE. Yes I would.

BLODWEN. Thought so.

JAYNE. Did you put something in it?

BLODWEN. No, love. You did.

BLODWEN *goes out to the kitchen, comes back with a bottle of whisky, tops up both teas.*

Allun's this is, from Christmas, he don't deserve it.

JAYNE. Who the hell is Allun?

BLODWEN. 'Who the hell is Allun'! That's my lovely. My mate. Bring you back to life, this. For now, like. I'm sorry on it.

BLODWEN *hands* JAYNE *her tea. She takes it gingerly.*

JAYNE. You could put poison in it!

BLODWEN. Are you on medication?

JAYNE. What for?

BLODWEN. Your – pain?

JAYNE. No!

BLODWEN. That's alright, then.

Pause.

You can stay y'here. I've decided. 'Til it comes for you, time. Don't mind them, they can lump off.

JAYNE. Are you going to kill me in my sleep?

Beat.

BLODWEN. Do you want me to?

JAYNE. No.

BLODWEN. When did you know? You was having to come back?

JAYNE. Very sudden.

BLODWEN. What a shock for you, though. It's a shock for me! I knew you'd come, mind. I just never knowed when. How long have you got?

JAYNE. Until tomorrow.

BLODWEN. Oh Christ. Oh, God love you, come y'here.

JAYNE. No.

BLODWEN. Alright, love. It's okay.

Pause.

I've a memory somewhere of the day you went.

JAYNE. Who are you talking about now?

BLODWEN. I'll find it. Curly hair you had then, wasn't it?

JAYNE. I had curly hair.

BLODWEN. That's how we got on. Same class, same hair. Two peas, one pod.

JAYNE. Who, me?

During the following, JAYNE *pulls up her tights.*

BLODWEN. We was in tall grass looking up at the sky. Bright, bright sky. Making stories of the clouds. They was coming together and drifting apart. Only you could hardly not tell it, 'cos the day were so still, like. We was the only ones in the world to notice. You had on that top, same colour as the tree. Brought out your wondering eye. Kiss curl by there. You said, 'If you ever forget me I will find you and kill you.' I said, 'Never', like as if I would, like. We made a memory of that on the air to take with you on your way. You said, 'If I don't see you before, I'll come back y'here to die. You can be the last to say hello.' You was always great for a promise. And now you've come back to me until tomorrow. 'Hello!'

JAYNE. 'Hello!'

BLODWEN. Pretend I'm not y'here, it's alright.

JAYNE. I thought you were going to kill me.

BLODWEN. I would! If you want it. I don't mind!

JAYNE. Come here.

JAYNE takes BLODWEN*'s wrist.*

Kill you with kindness.

BLODWEN. Don't say it! Don't you say that now, it's not right.

JAYNE. Say it.

BLODWEN. No I won't.

JAYNE. Say it.

BLODWEN. No I can't.

JAYNE. Kill you with kindness!

BLODWEN. Kill you with kindness.

They embrace.

JAYNE. I'm not here to die.

BLODWEN. You are, love. You are.

JAYNE. Not.

BLODWEN. I can't believe it.

JAYNE. It's my mother.

BLODWEN. What is?

JAYNE. My mother is dead.

BLODWEN. Oh Christ, love. Not her as well. It's all over like a rotten smell!

JAYNE. Listen to me. It's my mother. In the urn. That's why. Not me. I came to say goodbye to her. I came to let her go. Home. This was her home.

BLODWEN. I know that, don't I?

JAYNE. Oh yeah.

BLODWEN. You're not dying? Tomorrow, though?

JAYNE. No, not tomorrow.

BLODWEN. You weren't trying to throw yourself off?

JAYNE. No. I was trying to throw her off. I didn't manage it. I'll have to go tomorrow. Have that drink.

BLODWEN. Yes I would.

JAYNE. I thought you were going to kill me.

BLODWEN. I thought I were going to have to!

JAYNE. I must a bit pissed. I wanted to take her . . . You know. Well you know. I'm sure she would have wanted to come back. In the end. She didn't say. But. Bloody crematorium was deathly, not leaving her there. Not wearing even the right clothes. It's a sodding long way up there, you know.

BLODWEN. I know!

JAYNE. It doesn't look it to look at it. And then you have to come all the way down again. Got up there. Someone else would've gone through with it. I'd imagined more green. I just couldn't imagine her there. Ever. Alone. She was so. (*Beat*.) Loved. (*Beat*.) I couldn't even do that for her.

BLODWEN. Just you now, isn't it?

JAYNE. I did spill a bit though.

BLODWEN. Ah well. It all goes to make a turd.

JAYNE. So I bottled out. Came back down and got pissed. (*Beat*.) That's when I met you, wasn't it?

BLODWEN. I couldn't leave you with him, I know what he's like.

JAYNE. You rescued me.

BLODWEN. Spitty Del. Makes a change, don't it?

JAYNE. Does it? He did spit.

BLODWEN. Will I tell you a funny story?

JAYNE. Yes please.

BLODWEN. I were going up the Tick the other day, right. Oh Christ, I bumped into Mary. You'd never know her! She has no neck at all now and a very bad foot. She had that coming, mind. Duw. Anyhow, right. I'm in the post office for something for Em, I can't remember what it was now. My mind is a fart in a colander. But. So. I'm in the post shop and they've put up a sign see, see some circus up London. And I'm looking at it, and I don't know why. I never been up London. I'm thinking. I could just go up there. I could just go. And I'm thinking, even if I don't go up the circus, right, I might bump into Jayne! I swear to God, I were thinking it. And then I'm thinking even if I don't bump into Jayne, right, I could probably find her if she's there! 'Cos I am like that, me. I really did thought about doing that, I swear on my grave. (*Beat*.) That were only the other day and now you've come back until tomorrow!

JAYNE. That is funny.

Beat.

BLODWEN. How old's your mam, sixty-five?

JAYNE. Sixty-seven.

BLODWEN. Wood smoke, love her.

JAYNE *looks all around the floor for the urn, can't see it anywhere.*

JAYNE. Oh.

BLODWEN. What's the matter, love?

JAYNE. Oh God.

BLODWEN. You alright?

JAYNE. This would be typical, I don't believe it.

BLODWEN. You alright, love?

JAYNE. Shit! Sorry.

BLODWEN. What is it?

JAYNE. I've not lost her!

BLODWEN. Oh! Ah, love. I know. Come y'here.

JAYNE. No, I've lost her!

BLODWEN. She's gone to a better place.

JAYNE. What I've – ? How can I have lost her?

BLODWEN. Breaks my heart / to see you.

JAYNE. I was determined to be so. Where?

BLODWEN. We'll go tomorrow, I know the spot.

JAYNE. How can you lose – ?! / I don't understand.

BLODWEN. Well this is what they say. / You can't, love. It's too big. You just have to go through it.

JAYNE. What have I done?

BLODWEN. You mustn't blame yourself.

JAYNE. Well there's no one else to blame, is there?

JAYNE *spots the urn on top of the dresser.*

Is that her?

BLODWEN. No, love. She's gone.

JAYNE. Oh, thank God! She's up there!

BLODWEN. There's a lovely way to look on it.

JAYNE. What's she doing up there?

BLODWEN. She's probably having a beano!

JAYNE. I thought. Oh God, that's a relief!

BLODWEN. Ah, love. It'll bite you in the bum for now.

JAYNE. That's alright, it's fine, it's fine.

BLODWEN. There's brave you are. She'll be smiling down on you.

JAYNE. I thought I'd lost her!

BLODWEN. She'll be up there smiling.

JAYNE. D'you think?

BLODWEN. I do think. I do.

JAYNE. Christ, I am drunk.

Pause.

BLODWEN. It'll come over you like that. I seen my own mother go through it, never mind if she's a cow.

Pause.

JAYNE. I'm not feeling very well, actually.

BLODWEN. Let's get you out of them clothes.

BLODWEN *helps* JAYNE *remove her coat.* JAYNE *leans on* BLODWEN *as she removes her shoes, skirt, tights, and helps to extract her bra from under her blouse.*

D'you remember her making us make that macramé? Wouldn't let us out 'til we'd finished, did she? D'you remember? You reckoned yours wasn't as good as my one so you chucked it. You had high standards see, I never. I kept mine. Plant-pot holder.

JAYNE. Oh! (*Beat.*) Oh. (*Beat.*) Oh, the fucking macramé. (*She laughs.*) The fucking macramé. (*Laughs harder,* BLODWEN *joins in.*) The fucking macramé. (*Hysterical.*) The fucking macramé. The fucking macramé. (*She weeps.*)

BLODWEN *puts a blanket around* JAYNE, *tries to hold her.* JAYNE *pushes her away.*

BLODWEN. Come y'here.

JAYNE. No don't. I'm alright.

BLODWEN. No you don't, bloody girl. I'm not having it. Come y'here.

BLODWEN *rocks* JAYNE.

JAYNE. I mean. (*Beat.*) She wanted me to be.

BLODWEN. Thick as crocks, me.

JAYNE. What did you want to be when you grew up?

BLODWEN. I never wanted to be nothing, I don't think. Did I?

JAYNE. Happy?

BLODWEN. Oh Jesu-Lord-O-Man's-Desiring, you're not expecting much, are you?

JAYNE. It's such a disappointment. They should've said.

BLODWEN. Well. You have to have something to look forward to. (*Beat.*) D'you remember the Impossible Task? (*Beat.*) You made that up, you did.

JAYNE. Who? Me?

BLODWEN. We was on a trip, you just come out with it. You was always doing that.

JAYNE. Was I?

BLODWEN. And I'd say, 'Set us an Impossible Task!' And you'd say, 'Walk to the lip of the sea and find out the urchins. And step-stone across them over the water.' And I'd say, 'That's not impossible!' And you'd say, 'Until you reach the horizon.' (*Beat.*) They don't tell you that, do they? They don't tell you what you are. They tell you what you ought to be.

Pause.

JAYNE. Blodwen.

BLODWEN. Yes, love. I'm only up the wooden hill. I'll find you if you need me, right?

JAYNE. I think I might be sick.

BLODWEN. Right up. Expect the worst.

BLODWEN *goes to the kitchen, comes back with a bowl, places it by* JAYNE.

JAYNE. I don't drink, you see.

BLODWEN. I know. I know, love. I'm sorry on it.

BLODWEN *sits next to her, strokes her forehead. Hums a tune. Burps.*

Cucumber's lethal.

(*Singing.*) I wish I were a fascinating bitch
I'd never be poor
I'd always be rich
I'd live in a house
With a big red light

JAYNE. Go tomorrow.

BLODWEN.
I'd sleep all day
And I'd work all night

JAYNE. S' nice.

BLODWEN.

> And every now and then
> I'd take a holiday
> Just to make my customers wild
> I wish I were a fascinating bitch
> And not an illegitimate child.

Pause. BLODWEN *turns off two lamps and the fire. She takes the urn, places it outside the front door. She picks up* JAYNE*'s clothes.*

I'm only up the hill, right?

JAYNE. Blodwen.

BLODWEN. Yes, love?

JAYNE is asleep. Lights.

Scene Two

The following morning. JAYNE *is asleep on the sofa. The curtains are drawn, one lamp remains lit – the room is dark and gloomy. The sound of rain against the window.* BLODWEN *comes down the stairs, goes to front door, brings the urn in. She is dressed for work. She goes into the kitchen. The sound of a kettle being filled and tea being prepared.* BLODWEN *sings to the tune of 'By the Ashgrove' –*

BLODWEN (*offstage, singing*).

> Jayne Llewelyn is a funny-un
> She's got a face like a pickled onion
> She's got a nose like a squashed tomato
> And feet like roast beef.

She brings in a mug of tea and places it next to JAYNE. *Edges her way onto the sofa.*

JAYNE *stirs.*

Cup of tea there.

JAYNE. Right. Thanks.

BLODWEN. Do you take sugar or not?

JAYNE. Not.

BLODWEN. You asleep?

JAYNE. No. Fine.

BLODWEN. Ah, great. I have to go, I'm sorry. Another grey day. How's your head? I done your clothing. I got the worst off.

JAYNE. Why, what was wrong?

BLODWEN. You had a bit of an accident.

JAYNE. Oh.

BLODWEN. I'll find out times of trains for you while I'm there.

JAYNE. Yes, thanks.

BLODWEN. You'll be alright with Em, she's upstairs? I've told her you're y'here.

JAYNE. Right.

BLODWEN. She'll get on your tits but you won't mind her.

JAYNE. No. Okay.

BLODWEN. You'll not go nowhere, will you? I get home around three. Buggering good it is to see you.

JAYNE. Yeah. Have a good day. Blodwen.

BLODWEN. Ta, love.

BLODWEN *goes. Silence.*

JAYNE. Oh shit.

She drinks some tea, tries to pull herself together.

Oh shit.

She gets up and goes to the window, clutching the blanket. She can't cope with the light.

Oh God. Oh God.

She goes to her bag, rummages. Brings out a packet of painkillers, takes two.

Oh. God.

She puts on her clothes and sits. Takes a swig of her tea. Smells her skirt. She's sick all over her clothes.

Oh Christ.

JAYNE *goes out upstairs.*

Pause. EMILY *comes in from upstairs carrying the cat. Goes out to the kitchen. The sound of a kettle, the toilet flushes.* JAYNE *comes downstairs, holding a small towel about herself, as* EMILY *comes in from the kitchen.*

Oh, shit! Sorry. You made me jump!

Pause.

Who's this?

EMILY. Saucy.

JAYNE. Hello, Saucy.

EMILY. I'm putting her out, she needs a poo.

EMILY *goes out to the kitchen.*

JAYNE. Sake!

JAYNE *grabs the blanket and wraps it round herself.* JAYNE *puts her bra on.* EMILY *comes in, sees, goes out again.* JAYNE *sits, rubbing her face.*

EMILY (*offstage*). I'm doing you a tea.

EMILY *comes back in.*

JAYNE. Er. Oh. Your mum – Thanks. Should you be doing that? Making cups of tea with boiling water?

EMILY considers JAYNE. Pause. EMILY goes to the window and looks out at the sky.

So. You must be Emily.

EMILY stares blankly back at JAYNE.

I'm Jayne.

EMILY. I know.

JAYNE. Right. Great.

EMILY. How old *are* you? (*Beat.*) Mam said you was *old*.

JAYNE. Did she?

Pause.

EMILY. She said you was a right laugh.

Pause.

JAYNE. I'll make the tea.

EMILY. I'm doing it!

JAYNE. I'll go.

EMILY. Do you have sugar?

JAYNE. No!

EMILY. Alright! I'm not bothered!

JAYNE goes out to the kitchen.

JAYNE (*offstage*). Do you take sugar?

EMILY. Four.

JAYNE (*offstage*). Where d'you keep it anyway?

EMILY. Under the sink.

JAYNE comes in with a mug of tea.

JAYNE. Funny place to keep sugar.

EMILY. We got ants.

Pause. JAYNE *goes back to the kitchen.*

JAYNE (*offstage*). Oh God!

JAYNE *comes back, hobbling.*

I've trodden in something!

EMILY. Saucy.

JAYNE *goes out, upstairs.* EMILY *searches through* JAYNE*'s bag. Takes out her purse. Takes a twenty-pound note and pockets it. Puts the purse back, continues to search.* JAYNE *comes in.*

JAYNE. Don't even think about it!

EMILY. Alright!

Pause.

JAYNE. I need to borrow something. To wear.

EMILY. There's one over the bannister.

JAYNE *goes upstairs, taking her bag.* EMILY *finds the urn, goes to the front door, places it outside the front door.* JAYNE *comes back in, she is wearing* EMILY*'s dressing gown, which is far too small.*

JAYNE. I need something to go out in.

EMILY. What've you got that on for?

JAYNE. I had a bit of an accident.

EMILY. I seen the bowl. My dad's that is.

JAYNE. Can I borrow some clothes, Emily? To go out in. I have to go.

EMILY. Top of the stairs, I told you.

JAYNE. Oh, are there? I thought you meant this. Right.

JAYNE *goes out, upstairs.* EMILY *takes a key from the Welsh dresser and locks the front door.* JAYNE *comes in dressed in* BLODWEN*'s clothes from the night before.*

I'll post this back. You'll have to give me her name and address.

EMILY. I thought you knew her? Did she make that up?

JAYNE. Oh. That's right.

EMILY. She said you was an *old* friend. Did she?

JAYNE. What? I don't know.

EMILY. If you know her.

JAYNE. I don't remember.

EMILY. You sure?

There's a knock at the door. JAYNE *goes to open the door, finds it locked.* JAYNE *opens the letter box.*

JAYNE. Hello?

EMILY. There's nobody there.

JAYNE. There's nobody there.

EMILY. I know.

JAYNE. Somebody knocked.

EMILY. We've a ghost.

JAYNE. What – ?

EMILY. I said we got a ghost.

JAYNE. I have to go.

EMILY. You can't.

JAYNE. What?

EMILY. Door's locked.

JAYNE. Oh. Christ. Why did she do that?

EMILY. She always locks me in when I'm on my own.

JAYNE. What if there's a fire? There must be a key somewhere.

EMILY. What are you doing round y'here?

JAYNE. I had something to do.

EMILY. Most of the English round y'here's on holiday. Dad
  says they don't do nothing else.

JAYNE. Not me.

EMILY. You never come up to see my mam, did you?

JAYNE. We bumped into each other in the pub.

EMILY. Don't tell her.

JAYNE. What?

EMILY. You don't remember.

JAYNE. I know!

EMILY. Alright!

  Beat.

JAYNE. Don't tell her.

  Beat.

EMILY. D'you need some breakfast? I'm having poached eggs
  in vinegar, want one?

  Beat.

JAYNE. Yeah. Okay.

EMILY. Bara Brith or Hovis?

  Beat.

JAYNE. Hovis. Please.

EMILY. Right.

  EMILY *goes out.*

    (*Offstage, singing.*) I could work all day with a big red light
    I'd never be poor which would be alright
    I wish I were a fascinating child
    And not a little little little bitch . . .

This is clearly fingernails on a blackboard for JAYNE. *She goes through drawers in search of a key.*

Would you like one egg or would you like two eggs?

JAYNE. Two.

Pause.

EMILY (*offstage*). Would you like one slice of Hovis or would you like / two slice of Hovis?

JAYNE. Two slices, please.

Beat. EMILY *comes in, making* JAYNE *jump.*

EMILY. Would you like butter / or would you like margarine?

JAYNE. Oh God! Yes! Please. Butter, please. Do you want me to do it!

EMILY. No, it's alright.

EMILY *goes out.*

JAYNE. What time does your mum get in from work?

EMILY (*offstage*). About three if she doesn't go to the shop.

JAYNE. Oh God. I'm stuck here then, aren't I?

EMILY (*offstage*). Who were you visiting?

EMILY *comes out of the kitchen.*

If it weren't my mam?

JAYNE. Has she mentioned me before?

EMILY. You can't go without saying goodbye, I'd never hear the fucking end on it. Eggs!

EMILY *goes out to the kitchen.* JAYNE *has realised the urn is missing, she looks all over for it.*

JAYNE. Emily? Have you seen? It's like a pot, thing.

EMILY (*offstage*). What's it look like?

JAYNE. It's silver. It's not shiny. It's quite big, you can't miss it. I had it last night I think. I think – did your mum put it somewhere?

EMILY (*offstage*). She's always doing that. Will I help you look?

JAYNE. Would you?

They search – EMILY *goes upstairs,* JAYNE *looks in the dresser, etc.*

I can't see it anywhere.

EMILY (*offstage*). Me neither.

JAYNE. I can't have lost it, can I?

EMILY (*offstage*). She'll have it somewhere, I bet you. She's always doing it.

JAYNE. Jesus, if I've lost it! Can we phone her?

EMILY *comes back in.*

EMILY. It's only incoming calls. Dad's putting a stop to Mam's gassing.

JAYNE. You are joking.

EMILY. Not. He says it's not fucking funny any more.

JAYNE. Is there a call phone? Payphone, phone box?

EMILY. Last week it weren't working, anyhow. Mam tried to use it when she thought she'd won the lotto. You could phone from next door, but he's out on a morning.

JAYNE. What time's your mum back?

EMILY. She never tells me nothing. I promise you she'll have it safe, she's always doing it. Where are you meant to go?

Pause. JAYNE *is not eating.*

D'you want red sauce?

JAYNE. No thanks.

EMILY. D'you want brown sauce?

JAYNE. No.

EMILY. I like your hair. Who were you visiting?

JAYNE. No one.

EMILY. You're not too bright, are you?

JAYNE. I feel awful, actually. Just between you and me.

EMILY. You should have them eggs.

JAYNE. You're rushing yours. So we're locked in. You and me.

EMILY. And Saucy.

JAYNE. And Saucy.

EMILY. Saucy can have your eggs.

JAYNE starts to eat her eggs.

JAYNE. What do you want to do today, then?

There's a knock at the door.

EMILY. And the ghost.

JAYNE. Does it have a name?

EMILY. Rosemary.

JAYNE. Right. Is there anything you fancy doing?

EMILY. Not bothered.

JAYNE. What do you normally do?

EMILY (*shrugs*). Don't know.

Pause.

JAYNE. What do you want to be when you grow up?

EMILY. I just go on.

JAYNE. When you grow up?

EMILY. That's easy. I want to be an astronaut.

JAYNE. How original.

EMILY. What's original? I want to see a Sun Dog from above.

Pause.

JAYNE. What, God?

EMILY. Where? It's a cloud! It's a brilliant cloud.

JAYNE. Is it? Maybe that is God.

EMILY. I don't know.

JAYNE. No. Me neither.

EMILY. I could of showed you Puzzle Wood!

JAYNE. What's that?

EMILY. It's amazing, right. You go in, and there's loads of trees. And it's like a puzzle.

JAYNE. Like a maze?

EMILY. I don't know, I've never been to one.

JAYNE. Pointless exercise, they are. You go in and you walk round and round in sodding circles until you find the bench in the middle. Then you realise the time and you take all the wrong turns out again. (*Beat.*) Bit like life, really.

EMILY. Puzzle Wood's not like that.

JAYNE. I'd like to have seen it.

Pause.

EMILY. What is it, your pot?

JAYNE. What?

EMILY. Your urn? (*Beat.*) Is it?

Beat.

JAYNE. My mother.

EMILY. It's shit when they go.

JAYNE. Yes. Yes it is. It is. Shit. (*Beat*.) She used to live up the mountain. As a kid. She had a favourite spot. You know, where anything was possible.

EMILY. Is it?

JAYNE. Thought she could fly off it. If she needed, she said. She thought she could fly! She just never needed to. Or maybe . . . I just don't know! I don't know. I went up there yesterday. And everything she'd ever told me . . . was somewhere else. Not there. I thought, this can't be it? But I can't ask her . . . What if I've got it all wrong? Got a bit scared, actually. Plus I don't like heights. Pathetic really.

EMILY. You can have a cry.

JAYNE *laughs*.

She sounds nice, your mam.

JAYNE. She was. (*Beat*.) What do Mum and Dad normally do with you? You're a bit young to be left before now.

EMILY. No, I normally go up Nana Evans, but she's died now of tumours.

JAYNE. Oh.

EMILY. That's her clock, look. Lonely it is. She had a right funny name, Nana Evans.

JAYNE. What was that?

EMILY. Nest!

JAYNE. Nest Evans?

EMILY. She used to say I'd gone home to roost!

Beat.

JAYNE. Do you miss her?

EMILY. No! 'Cos when I miss her, I just remember. She used to say – 'Em, we're going to make a memory!'

JAYNE. Did she?

EMILY. Clock's lonely 'cos it can't make none.

JAYNE. She sounds wonderful.

EMILY. She is. My mam calls photos 'memories'. D'you think that's daft?

JAYNE. No.

EMILY gets paper and pens from the sideboard and starts to draw.

EMILY. I'm doing you a picture.

JAYNE. You don't have to.

EMILY. I am. I'm doing you a picture of your spot. It's the sea. And that's the sky. And it's shining, the sun is, so you can't see no planets. And that's you, that is. There. J-A-N-E.

There's a knock at the door. JAYNE turns to the door.

JAYNE. There's a 'Y' in Jayne.

EMILY. Where?

JAYNE turns back.

JAYNE. There.

EMILY. Why?

Beat.

JAYNE. Why not?

Lights.

Scene Three

Later the same day. JAYNE and EMILY have made a tent in the living room out of sheets and towels, a clothes horse, etc. They're sitting inside it. EMILY holds a torch and is shining it into JAYNE's face. They're laughing.

JAYNE. Right so, what you have to do is, you take a smile, right? You wipe it off your face like this and scrunch it up tightly, and you blow it to the other person. And the other person catches it and puts it on. Right? – that's you. And you wear the smile for as long as you want, but you have to make sure it's a really, really big smile or it's not going to work, and then you take the smile off and blow it back to me.

EMILY. How do you know all these games?

JAYNE. I have absolutely no idea. Right?

EMILY. Right.

JAYNE. Oh, and all the time that I've got the smile on, you're not allowed to smile, and all the time you've got the smile on I'm not allowed to smile. Got it?

EMILY. Have you got a sister?

JAYNE. No, why?

EMILY. Just wondered. Have you got a brother?

JAYNE. No. No mum. No dad. No brother. No sister. Just me.

EMILY. And me.

JAYNE. And you. Now. Ready?

EMILY. You go first.

JAYNE. Right.

JAYNE *puts a smile on her face and grins from ear to ear like a fool.* EMILY *finds this hilarious.*

No, you berk! You're not meant to smile.

EMILY. I can't help it. You look a twat!

JAYNE. Yeah. Well. That is kind of the point. Now, wipe that smile off and chuck it here, fart face.

EMILY. Alright!

EMILY *tries to look as serious as she possibly can.* JAYNE *puts the smile on and tries again. She ignores* EMILY's

reaction which of course is to smile, and blows the smile to
EMILY. EMILY *puts it on and grins.* JAYNE *laughs.*
EMILY *laughs.*

JAYNE. Well that's not going to work is it?

EMILY. No! Do it again!

JAYNE. Alright. (*Beat.*) I am going to have to go back today,
Em. You know?

EMILY. Have you got a computer?

JAYNE. Yeah!

EMILY. Who d'you talk to on it?

JAYNE. Just people. It never seems real, somehow.

EMILY. Why not?

JAYNE. Well. It's behind a screen. You can't touch it. It's like
talking to the air.

EMILY. You can't touch talking! Talking is air.

JAYNE. True. Hot air.

EMILY. Hot air balloon!

JAYNE. Hot air balloon with streamers.

EMILY. And ribbons!

JAYNE. Carrying a giraffe.

EMILY. With its head in the clouds!

JAYNE. On an air pocket.

EMILY. Into space! (*Beat.*) I don't want you to go. Do you
have to?

JAYNE. I don't know where I am here. (*Beat.*) I'd like to go
into space with you. And I get vertigo! Big time!

EMILY. What's vertigo?

JAYNE. I told you, didn't I? Fear of heights.

EMILY. Oh yeah. Well you can't come then, can you? (*Beat.*)
     Why have you not got a boyfriend?

JAYNE. How do you know I haven't?

EMILY. I haven't. I don't.

JAYNE. I don't know, Em. I don't know. It wasn't his fault.
     There was lots of love. I wanted him to be. Someone else.

     Beat.

EMILY. You can have Allun!

JAYNE. Where is he today?

EMILY. Fishing.

JAYNE. Didn't you want to go with him?

EMILY. He says I'll hold him up.

JAYNE. Oh. Well you would, wouldn't you? It's such a fast
     sport!

EMILY. It's not! S'alright. I'm hanging out with you. This is the
     most fun I've had all holidays!

JAYNE. Can I let you into a secret? Me too!

EMILY. Can I let you into a secret?

JAYNE. Go on.

     Pause.

EMILY. Hot air.

JAYNE. Come on, we're going out!

EMILY. It's raining.

JAYNE. Well get your welly-blogs on, then. We're going to
     make a memory.

EMILY. We can't get out the house!

JAYNE. We'll climb out the window!

EMILY. It's the wrong bloody way!

JAYNE. No it's bloody not! It's a different way. It's the way
that leads to adventure. D'you know anything about dens?

EMILY. Not really . . .

JAYNE. Right then. We're going to make a proper den, me and
you. It's going to have a roof and a drawbridge and a bloody
great moat the way it's going. We're going to make a den to
end all dens. We'll make the best bloody den in the whole of
Welsh Wales!

EMILY. Is that alright?

JAYNE. Get your coat on. If you don't know where you're
going, all paths lead there. We're going on a lion hunt!

EMILY. What?

JAYNE. Say it.

EMILY. We're going on a lion hunt.

JAYNE. But we're not scared.

EMILY. But we're not scared.

JAYNE. 'Cos we've got guns. Bullets. Weeee!

*They both climb out of the window. Pause. EMILY climbs
back in, coat in hand, runs into the kitchen. JAYNE puts her
head through the window.*

Em?

*EMILY runs out of the kitchen with two oranges and two
biscuits, gives one of each to JAYNE through the window.*

EMILY. We might want these if we're building.

JAYNE. Good thinking.

EMILY. Can you take my skin off?

JAYNE. Course.

EMILY. How many N's in 'innate'?

JAYNE. How the hell do you know that?

EMILY. What?

JAYNE. 'Innate'?

EMILY. I don't know, I just know it.

JAYNE. Bloody hell! Two. We came across a mountain.

EMILY. We came across a mountain.

JAYNE. We couldn't go round it.

EMILY. We couldn't go round it.

JAYNE. We couldn't go through it.

EMILY. We couldn't go through it.

JAYNE. We'll have to go over it!

EMILY. We'll have to go over it!

> JAYNE *helps* EMILY *climb back out through the window.*
> *Silence. We hear a car pull up. The handle on the front door*
> *goes. A key in the lock.* EMILY *comes back in, defeated.*
> BLODWEN *follows, laden with bags of shopping. The urn is*
> *under her arm.*

BLODWEN. What the cow in hell's name is that bloody door
doing locked? Emily Evans!

EMILY. I don't know!

JAYNE. Alright?

BLODWEN. Alright, love? What do you have to say for yourself?

EMILY. Nothing.

BLODWEN. I'm not having it, bloody girl. We have a visitor!
What is it she's supposed to think?

JAYNE. What's – ? What's happened?

BLODWEN. She's locked the cowing frigging twat of a bloody
front door on you! It's a disgrace! I will twat you round the
lugs for that, I swear on it. Come y'here.

EMILY. I never!

JAYNE *sees the urn.*

JAYNE. Where was it?

BLODWEN. Just now, look.

EMILY. No!

JAYNE. Where did you find it?

BLODWEN. What?

EMILY. I never!

JAYNE. The urn!

BLODWEN. In the pub where you left it. Come y'here!

JAYNE. Blodwen, God's sake. I locked the door. Alright?
Sorry. It was me. With a hangover.

EMILY. Jayne done it.

JAYNE. Sorry.

BLODWEN. S'alright, love. I'm not having a do for you. It's
her. She's a bundle of fucking burden. What do you think
you're playing at?

EMILY. Nothing.

JAYNE. I can't believe I left her in the pub! I don't remember
doing that.

BLODWEN. You had your dinner?

EMILY. No. We was going out.

BLODWEN. Well have it now, then.

EMILY. Jayne's been telling us all stories on when you was my
age, haven't you?

JAYNE. Yes.

EMILY. We've had a right laugh. We're going on a lion hunt.

JAYNE. We're going on a lion hunt.

BLODWEN. You are not going on a buggering nowhere.

EMILY. We are!

BLODWEN. You're having your something to eat!

EMILY. I don't want any.

BLODWEN. You will!

EMILY. I don't.

BLODWEN. Emily Evans, get in that cowing kitchen now, and do yourself your bloody dinner! You're always buggering asking it!

EMILY *trudges off to the kitchen and closes the door.*

Takes after her father, that one. She's 'spludge' and he's 'streak'! Cupboard love it is, that's all, I'm not bloody having it.

JAYNE. I think that is quite possibly the worst thing I have ever done.

BLODWEN. They had it safe. Now look, this'll cheer you up. Train is at three so you've missed it.

JAYNE. Oh. Right.

BLODWEN. So what I've done, right. I've booked you a taxi for the morning if you need to go, and I've brung us in a beano!

JAYNE. Wow. Right.

BLODWEN *starts unpacking the bags.*

BLODWEN. We got . . . What've we got . . . We got . . . I brought you some more of the lovely stuff.

BLODWEN *produces a bottle of whisky.*

And what we don't drink now you can take home, see? And I got us some fizzy wine! And I got us some brandy in case we run out. And food! I got you Scotch eggs, 'cos I know how much you love them. And some liquorice sticks and a lovely drop of bacon. And. Oh that's just bread, that's boring that is.

And bog roll. And I've treated us to a cake! And I got some more butter, but you don't want to know about that. I'll just shove these.

JAYNE. Blodwen!

BLODWEN. No you bloody don't, bloody girl! You'll hurt my feelings!

JAYNE. I could get a cab / to another station . . .

BLODWEN. I'll just shove these.

BLODWEN *goes into the kitchen.*

(*Offstage.*) Something fucking stinks in this kitchen, and it's not bloody me!

EMILY (*offstage*). Mam – ?

BLODWEN *comes out, closing the door on* EMILY.

BLODWEN. She's not having it! It's just for us. Will I do you one now?

JAYNE. Oh God. It's a slippery slope, isn't it?

BLODWEN. Christ, bloody girl, it's an occasion! What's the matter with you? You used to be a bad influence!

JAYNE. Alright. But with water. Let's put some water in it.

JAYNE *goes to her bag, takes out a bottle of water.*

BLODWEN. There you go, look.

JAYNE. Just one. I really ought to go. And do the deed.

BLODWEN. Too late for all that now. Sun'll shine on the other side in the morning.

JAYNE. God, I was drunk last night, wasn't I?

BLODWEN. Out of your pod, love. You was smashing.

JAYNE. Cheers.

BLODWEN. Kill you with kindness!

JAYNE. Kill you with kindness?

BLODWEN. I'm kicking off these shoes 'cos they smell. How've you been, love?

JAYNE. Er. Great. Actually.

BLODWEN. Last thing you need's to get lumbered with her. She's worse than a bloody period!

JAYNE. What do you want her to be?

BLODWEN. Nothing.

EMILY *opens the kitchen door, she's out of breath.*

EMILY. Mam – ?

BLODWEN. I'm having my friend to tea, leave it out.

EMILY. I was just going to ask / if you wanted a cuppa?

BLODWEN. It's always asking, innit? Ask ask ask. And no, I don't.

EMILY. Right.

BLODWEN. If I want a tea I'll tell you, don't I? What you having, beans?

EMILY. Beans, yeah.

BLODWEN. Right then.

EMILY. Right.

EMILY *goes back into the kitchen and closes the door.*

BLODWEN. You hungry?

JAYNE. No. Fine.

BLODWEN. She fed you, did she?

JAYNE. She was very kind.

BLODWEN. Right. Or there'd be trouble. In the camp. Oh, innit nice being home?

JAYNE. Is it?

BLODWEN. Innit, though.

JAYNE. Will I get to meet Allun later?

BLODWEN. I hope not. He'll be up round Angharad's.

JAYNE. Will he take Emily?

BLODWEN. Fat chance. I'm y'here, aren't I?

EMILY *comes out of the kitchen with a plate of baked beans.*

EMILY. D'you want some?

JAYNE. No, love.

EMILY. They're cold?

JAYNE. Thank you.

BLODWEN. She's not having your beans! What d'you think she is, good for nothing?

JAYNE. I do like beans, actually.

BLODWEN. D'you want some?

EMILY. D'you want some?

JAYNE. No.

Pause.

BLODWEN. She's a big slimy piece of smelly turd.

EMILY *looks up.* JAYNE *looks at* BLODWEN.

JAYNE. How was work?

BLODWEN. Bloody hard work! She's alright on her cowing holidays! I couldn't wait to get back to you.

EMILY. Mam! Catch this smile –

BLODWEN *stares blankly back at* EMILY.

BLODWEN. Oh Christ, I don't believe it!

JAYNE. What?

EMILY. What, Mam?

BLODWEN. I left your fucking sanitary pads on the counter!

Beat.

EMILY. S'alright.

JAYNE. Oh. No.

BLODWEN. It is not bloody alright, is it?

EMILY. I don't need it.

BLODWEN. I'm not having her all over the shop. I'll have to go back.

EMILY. Don't worry, Mam.

BLODWEN. I've paid on it!!! I won't be long, love, is there anything you need?

JAYNE. No no. I'm absolutely fine.

BLODWEN. Right. You try a thing, bloody girl! I'll not be long.

JAYNE. Okay.

BLODWEN *goes. Car lights. Sound goes.*

You alright?

EMILY. I got Hefyn the Tall to phone you a taxi. It'll be y'here now.

JAYNE. What? When did you do that?

EMILY. When I was out the back. I climbed out the window and shouted up for him. You need to know where you are.

JAYNE. You are very lovely, Emily Evans.

EMILY. I want to tell you a secret before you go?

JAYNE. Okay. That's alright.

EMILY. Allun's doing Angharad.

Beat.

JAYNE. Your dad?

EMILY. Allun. He's doing my aunt.

Beat.

JAYNE. How do you know?

EMILY. I seen them last night.

JAYNE. Did you?

EMILY. I'm not lying.

JAYNE. I know. (*Beat.*) How?

EMILY. I'm not telling you.

JAYNE. And your mum doesn't know?

EMILY. You know.

JAYNE. Okay. (*Beat.*) Okay. (*Beat.*) What are you going to do?

EMILY. Nothing.

JAYNE. Do you want me to do something?

Car headlights across the window.

EMILY. That's your taxi. I have money for it.

EMILY *tries to give the twenty-pound note back to* JAYNE – *she doesn't take it.*

Take it up Aber, it'll take you up London.

JAYNE *goes to her purse, takes out a fiver. Gives it to* EMILY.

JAYNE. Tell them I'm ever so sorry. Okay? I'm sorry I troubled them. Tell them it was a mistake. I'm not going anywhere. Right?

EMILY. Right. (*Beat.*) I love you.

EMILY *goes out.* JAYNE *watches her go. The car headlights disappear – no* EMILY. *Pause.*

JAYNE. Emily?

Pause.

Em?!

Pause.

Em!!!

Silence.

Lights.

End of Act One.

ACT TWO

Scene One

Minutes later. JAYNE *is pacing the room.*

JAYNE. Oh shit. Oh God. Oh shit. Oh God. Oh Jesus. Jesus
Christ.

BLODWEN *appears in the doorway, carrying sanitary
towels.*

Oh shit! Sorry. You made me jump!

BLODWEN. You made me jump!

JAYNE. Sorry. / Did you see her?

BLODWEN. Mad. Who? The cat's mother?

JAYNE. She's gone, Blod.

BLODWEN. Ah, love. You having a wave?

JAYNE. You didn't see her, did you?

BLODWEN. No, love. I can't. Can you?

JAYNE. She just went.

BLODWEN. You seen her, did you?

JAYNE. I was talking to her – Aren't you worried?

BLODWEN. I am, love. I am worried right up. She's done it
before, hasn't it?

JAYNE. Has she?

BLODWEN. Last night. You don't remember, do you?

JAYNE. I thought she was at Angharad's.

BLODWEN. Right, love. Okay now, look. Let's get you out of them clothes and feet up, I'm doing it. You need to dream for big thoughts.

BLODWEN *tries to undress* JAYNE.

JAYNE. What are you doing? Blodwen. Stop it. Blodwen. Stop it!

JAYNE *pushes* BLODWEN *away.*

Just listen. To me. She's gone off with a complete stranger.

BLODWEN. She's gone to a better place!

JAYNE. Where – ? Oh, for God's sake. Not my mother, you bloody daft bloody cow! Em!

BLODWEN. Who?

JAYNE. Emily. Emily!

BLODWEN. When?

JAYNE. In a taxi!

BLODWEN. Where?

JAYNE. I don't bloody know, do I?

BLODWEN. Keep your hair on if your head blows up. What's she doing in a taxi?

JAYNE. She climbed out the window.

BLODWEN. What's she doing that for?

JAYNE. She had good reason, actually.

BLODWEN. She always has good reason.

JAYNE. Has she done this before?

BLODWEN. She's always buggering doing it. That's how come he takes her up Angharad's. She's never climbed out of there. She's done it deliberate so I'd have your nose rubbed all up it. I can't lock her in, can I? She'd probably cause a fire. I'd come home to a burnt house and a burnt daughter. Then what would they say?

JAYNE. But she'll come back.

BLODWEN. I give her twenty minties. You'll hear her coming a mile off, she'll be guzzling a tub of double cream. So. No. See. So. Will we have that fizzy wine, we should be celebrating? I have you for myself now, don't I?

BLODWEN goes out to the kitchen.

JAYNE. She. Told me a secret. Emily did.

BLODWEN (*offstage*). She hasn't got none.

JAYNE. Well. It's more yours, really. I'm probably not supposed to know.

BLODWEN (*offstage*). I'm all ears!

JAYNE. She said. Allun . . . is doing Angharad.

The sound of a cork popping in the kitchen. BLODWEN *comes out with wine and glasses.*

BLODWEN. He's been doing her for the past three years! That's what I mean, she's a big slimy piece of smelly turd. Always was. Only thing ever stopped her's you! And you went!

JAYNE. You knew.

BLODWEN. I might be daft but I'm not a twat. I found that out in a dream. I dreamt he was in marigolds to his waist. Nowhere round y'here, like. Beautiful, he looks, never mind his teeth. And in comes her. Smug as a cow giving suck. And they're all spitty and smiles. That were my dream, that were. I woke up and I goes, 'You'll never guess what,' and I told him. And Allun goes, 'Who's been talking to you?' (*Beat.*) There was a rumour last year he was putting it in the bacon slicer. Her that runs the butcher's round the mountain. How low can you go? (*Beat.*) Saves me a job, anyhow. I've never been into sex. It's too sticky for my liking. (*Beat.*) I just hope he gives her crickets.

Beat.

JAYNE. Crabs.

BLODWEN. Crabs, is it? At least he's from under my feet. All's he can do is pick holes and find farts. I can't even call up my own mother, look, from my own front room. Never mind if she's a cow.

JAYNE. Bit extreme, that.

BLODWEN. Extreme it is, innit? Extremely harsh. Frig-a-bloody-doon.

BLODWEN *goes out to the kitchen.*

JAYNE. Well I think you should leave him. Anyway. That's what I think.

BLODWEN (*offstage*). He told me to shove trees up my arse the other day.

JAYNE. You see? What the hell does he see in her, anyway?

BLODWEN (*offstage*). I know! She's so anal she'd clean the toilets on a train.

JAYNE. Well there you are!

EMILY *arrives at the doorway.*

Upstairs. Now!

EMILY *goes.* BLODWEN *comes in with a plate of things to nibble on.*

BLODWEN. I'm alright, I set my sights low, see. Sometimes I have a fancy I'll meet someone up the button shop.

JAYNE. Do you?

BLODWEN. D'you remember making us swap names? Swapping names all the bloody time, wasn't we though? You was Blod and I were Jayne. 'Why put the 'Y' in Jayne?'

JAYNE. 'Why not!' / Oh! Jesus!

BLODWEN. You reckoned Angharad couldn't touch me if I were you, you are good. I'd get six of the best with her hairbrush bristles when I got home, she always dobbed us in. Sat

with me for hours, you did, stroking my neck and crying.
You blamed yourself 'cos I were Jayne. You was always
crying over me.

JAYNE. I never cry.

BLODWEN. You do! Your mam used to say, 'Don't mind
Jayne, she don't know her own strength,' and you was
always bloody in tears!

JAYNE. Why was I always crying?

BLODWEN. Don't ask me, I can hardly tell the time. I had an
excuse for crying, see! Golden twat! Not your fault, love.
Not your fault she only had you.

JAYNE. Will you tell that to Emily?

BLODWEN. What's it got to do with her? I always wanted
your hair. Lust I had, for your hair. Your curls made sense,
mine never. Where did they go? Beautiful, it is. Straight and
lush and bright. And when the wind blows, you float with it,
don't you?

JAYNE. I can't do a thing with my hair.

BLODWEN. Beautiful. And look at this thing. Look at this
dirty mop of Brillo. Unlucky with that, aren't I? It's no
wonder. I found you under a sunflower.

There's a crash in the kitchen.

You cow on a stalk!

BLODWEN *goes out to the kitchen.*

JAYNE. It means something, 'Blodwen', doesn't it?

BLODWEN (*offstage*). White flower. You've a memory.

JAYNE. D'you want me to go round and sort Angharad out?

BLODWEN (*offstage*). You have better to do than flap.

There's a knock at the door. BLODWEN *comes in.*

Ignore her. You'll need your silence when you get home.

JAYNE. I can't stand silence. It's like a black hole.

BLODWEN. What did I come in the room for?

> BLODWEN *sees the sanitary towels.*

> I'll just shove these.

> BLODWEN *goes upstairs. Silence.* EMILY *comes in. She has plastered her hair with Vaseline.*

JAYNE. Em? Jesus. What have you done to your hair?

EMILY. D'you like it?

JAYNE. Sweetheart. What've you done?

EMILY. I put Vaseline over it.

JAYNE. Oh for God's sake.

> JAYNE *goes to her bag, and takes out make-up bag, hair-brush, etc.*

> Sit on the floor there, look.

> EMILY *sits on the floor.* JAYNE *sits behind her on the sofa.*

> Hold this.

> *She hands* EMILY *a hand mirror – they talk to each other through the reflection.*

> You're going to have to have this cut, Em. We won't get it out, just washing it. What the hell were you trying to do?

EMILY. Make it straight like yours. It makes you float and shine. Will I have to wear a wig?

JAYNE. That's what you get for listening at doors. No. You'll just have to wear it short. It'll grow. That's the thing about hair.

EMILY. Will I look stupid?

JAYNE. What do you think?

EMILY. I look stupid.

JAYNE. Where did you go?

EMILY. Do I look like Blodwen?

JAYNE. A bit.

EMILY. Do I look like Blodwen when she was nine?

JAYNE. I suppose so.

EMILY. You don't remember, do you? I forgot.

JAYNE. Keep still.

EMILY. Will I look like Blodwen at your age?

JAYNE. What would you like to look like at my age?

EMILY. I don't want to look like my mam. I went and found my spot. Like your mam had.

JAYNE. She was worried.

EMILY. She was never.

JAYNE. How do you know?

EMILY. I know! Alright? (*Beat.*) I didn't feel like flying. I didn't want to go nowhere. I watched my breath go out on the night air then I come back. I'll know where it is when I need to go.

JAYNE. You have to tell someone where you're going.

EMILY. No, 'cos then it'd never be my spot! I only come back to say goodbye to you, I wish I'd never bothered!

JAYNE. Don't be so bloody stupid!

EMILY. Alright!

Pause.

JAYNE. You'll look like you. No one else. Just you. No just. You. You might remind people of your mum.

EMILY. What did you want to look like when you growed up?

JAYNE. No such thing, Em. There's no such thing as growing up. There's only growing older. Time passing. The trick is working out what you do in the meanwhile.

Pause.

What does your spaceship look like?

EMILY. I'm not bothered!

JAYNE. Be bothered! It's your spaceship, nobody else's. What do spaceships need?

EMILY. Ask ask ask! Windows. So you can see where you're going.

JAYNE. Go on.

EMILY. Alright! They're round, right. So you can fit a whole planet in the view.

JAYNE. And?

EMILY. Ask! Spaceship's round so I fit in with the planets. I'm painting it pink, then you'll see me coming. But not a reddy pink, a pinkish pink, or I'll look like Mars and if I bump into someone they might try to land on me.

JAYNE. You don't want that?

EMILY. No! I'll have to have a machine to talk to Earth for when I want to come back. And lots of straws coming out of cupboards full of juice.

JAYNE. Are you going to take anything with you?

EMILY. Mushy biscuits.

JAYNE. Apart from bloody food!

EMILY. All the things I've learned on Earth and when I find the aliens I can tell them – I'll tell them all about you. I'll tell them to pray for Jayne because she's sad, they can send a shooting star to brighten you up – you doing my hair or what?

Pause.

In space, right. At night it's not even black because of the stars and because of the moon. And in the day, it's all white. Like that sheet is. And you can start all over again.

JAYNE. I'm afraid to say, it's always black in space. Get used to it. You'll just have to keep going.

EMILY. Only until I find the white! You think you know everything!

Pause.

JAYNE. My spaceship . . . I'm afraid of heights.

EMILY. No heights in space.

JAYNE. No atmosphere.

EMILY. To cut with a knife.

JAYNE. Okay. My spaceship. Is a triangle. I'm bang in the centre. I can go up, or left or right. But not down. I'm going to paint it . . . the same colour as the sky. Then nobody knows I'm there.

EMILY. I won't be able to find you.

JAYNE. No one will. I'll put a really bright light on each tip of the triangle. If I see you, I'll flash. I'll have to have loads of cupboards with loads of supplies because I'm not going to be able to come back if I can't go down. I'll have to live on rations. So I'll probably get really thin which'll be good. Except that no one'll be able to see me. I'll just whizz about for the rest of my days trying to reach infinity.

BLODWEN *comes downstairs. She pauses to watch.*

EMILY. Infinity makes my head hurt.

JAYNE. Me too. Maybe I'll find the cure for that and beam it back telepathically.

EMILY. What the buggering hell is that?

JAYNE *stares hard at* EMILY *in the mirror, communicating her thoughts.* EMILY *laughs.*

JAYNE. How's that?

EMILY. I look funny.

JAYNE. Better than nothing, isn't it? You look like someone who could grow up to be an astronaut. Shall we have a cup of tea?

EMILY. You can make it.

JAYNE. Okay.

JAYNE *goes out to the kitchen.* BLODWEN *comes in, hits* EMILY *across the head.*

BLODWEN. What the fuck have you done to your head?

EMILY. Nothing.

BLODWEN. Don't give me that, you little cow! What's your bloody father have to say? Your hair's the only thing you had going now. What the frigging hell's bloody name d'you think you've gone and done?

EMILY. Jayne done it.

BLODWEN. Jayne done it, did she? You cow!

BLODWEN *hits* EMILY. JAYNE *comes out of the kitchen.*

Jayne done it? Let me tell you, you girl. Jayne would not do something like that!

JAYNE. Blodwen, calm down.

BLODWEN. And d'you want to know why? 'Cos she's not thick, that's why. She's not stupid.

JAYNE. Blodwen.

BLODWEN. And she wouldn't make a tit of it like you do, would she?

JAYNE. Blod. Stop it.

BLODWEN. Don't stick up for it, the little cow. Come y'here, I want to slap your legs.

JAYNE *gets in between the two of them.*

JAYNE. I did do her hair.

BLODWEN *lunges at* EMILY.

BLODWEN. No she didn't.

JAYNE *slaps* BLODWEN.

JAYNE. I did do it. It's my fault.

BLODWEN *lunges at* EMILY.

BLODWEN. No she wouldn't.

JAYNE *slaps* BLODWEN.

JAYNE. I did do it.

BLODWEN *lunges at* EMILY.

BLODWEN. She didn't.

JAYNE. I did.

JAYNE *punches* BLODWEN. *She falls to the floor.*

Emily. Go upstairs.

EMILY. I'm alright.

JAYNE. Emily. Get up those bloody stairs now, and get in your bloody bedroom!

EMILY. Alright! I'm not bothered.

EMILY *goes – she hovers in the doorway, unseen.*

JAYNE. I don't know who the hell you think you are. But you have no right. To fuck up. That child.

BLODWEN. She's my child.

JAYNE. I don't care. You haven't even acknowledged the fact she's come home! All she wants is to please you!

BLODWEN. She can't.

JAYNE. And who's fault is that? She wanted to look like me. So she'd please you.

BLODWEN. She's not normal.

JAYNE. She's a kid, / Blodwen! You are stealing all her hope.
Oh for God's sake –

BLODWEN. I wanted to look like you. I wanted to be you.

JAYNE. Grow up! Jesus. Christ. You don't know me! How can
you? How the hell can you possibly want to look like me or
be like me when you don't know who I am?

BLODWEN. I do know you.

JAYNE. You don't.

BLODWEN. I do know you, / you're beautiful.

JAYNE. I don't even recognise the person you're describing in
me! I don't know the person that stuck up for you. You
know, I just don't! The 'Kill you with kindness' – what the
hell does that mean? Swapping bloody names – I hate.
Loathe. And detest. Scotch eggs!

There's a knock at the door.

Fuck off, Rosemary! I'm this, I'm that – I'm the person who
left her own mother's remains in some pub!!! You know, you
prostrate yourself across my shadow and I don't even know
who you are! I don't remember you.

Pause.

I thought you'd come back to me but you haven't. (*Beat.*) I
don't remember you.

There's a knock on the door. JAYNE *turns and sees* EMILY.

I'm sorry.

BLODWEN. Forget it.

Beat.

JAYNE. I'm sorry.

BLODWEN. It's alright, love. It's okay.

JAYNE. It isn't.

BLODWEN *goes to the stairs, passing* EMILY.

BLODWEN. She needs Nana Evans.

BLODWEN *goes upstairs*.

EMILY. You don't know your own strength. (*Beat*.) I told you not to tell her. (*Beat*.) Will I tell you a funny story? This lady comes to the door and knocks. I goes to the door. No one's around to notice. She's nice looking. A lovely coat. I goes, 'Hello.' She goes, 'Hello.' I goes, 'What is it you are after?' She goes, 'I'd like to take a look around and see if this is somewhere I would like to be, I'm needing a place to stay.' I goes, 'You can't stay y'here, it's haunted!' She goes, 'Haunted, is it? By who?' I puts my face right up close to hers so no one else will hear it. And I goes . . . . 'You!' You touch my mam again and I will twat you round the lugs, I'm not having it. (*Beat*.) How did you feel when your mam died?

EMILY *goes upstairs*.

JAYNE. Like there was nothing left between me and the sky.

Lights.

Scene Two

Late that night. JAYNE *is on the settee, unable to sleep*. BLODWEN *comes downstairs*.

BLODWEN. You awake?

JAYNE. Yeah.

BLODWEN. Thought so. I have something for you.

JAYNE. Blod, I'm so sorry –

BLODWEN. I'm not having sorry! I'm not having it. There.

BLODWEN *hands* JAYNE *a photograph*.

I knew I had a memory somewhere. Proof.

JAYNE *takes the photograph. Studies it. Looks at*
BLODWEN. *Goes back to the photograph.*

JAYNE. Is that?

BLODWEN. May Day. It was under the bed.

JAYNE. You and me?

BLODWEN. In the sun.

JAYNE. That doesn't look like me at all.

BLODWEN. You haven't changed.

JAYNE. Does it look like you? No.

BLODWEN. I put on a bit of weight, like.

JAYNE. Look at the hair blowing over. It's like we've got the
same hair. We could be anybody.

BLODWEN. I knew I had that somewhere. It's where to look.
(*Beat.*) That's all I have of you.

JAYNE. Oh Blod. Oh. Blod. Blod. I am so sorry.

BLODWEN. Do yourself a favour and shut your gob, love. You
can have that.

JAYNE. I don't understand.

BLODWEN. No. And it's no cowing wonder, I never done you
nothing, did I? D'you want a cup of tea?

JAYNE. I'll make it.

BLODWEN. You stay where you are.

BLODWEN *goes out and busies herself in the kitchen.*
JAYNE *studies the photograph, deeply disturbed.*

JAYNE. Oh God.

BLODWEN (*offstage*). And where the cow is He when you
needs Him? In a fucking book and nowhere to be found.

JAYNE *strokes the photograph.*

JAYNE. You're smiling.

BLODWEN (*offstage*). I were with you, weren't I?

JAYNE. I look bloody miserable / – that is me, that one, isn't it?

BLODWEN (*offstage*). You weren't! You was tired up, we'd just had a laughing match. You blot out what you don't want, don't you?

BLODWEN *comes in with tea.*

You was sick that day with the whooping cough. I went with you up the nurse. She give you syrup. You said it tasted of poison. I tried to take some too, but you wasn't having it. Said, 'It'll make you sick.' In between the coughing, like. I said, 'I don't mind. If you have to have it, I have to have it.' That were good for your cough that stuff were, you threw it down the sink. You didn't care, you was trying to save me from harm. (*Beat.*) You was very caring.

Beat.

JAYNE. I –

BLODWEN. No, let me finish. You was also a twat from hell, mind.

JAYNE. That doesn't surprise me.

BLODWEN. D'you remember – no, you don't. There was one day, right. You took my knickers down and chucked me in a pale of roses and sat on it. I screamed the cowing houses down. No good reason, mind, that I can remember. You was just angried up with the world. Your mam always said you felt too much. Little girl. With all that hope. I never had that, see. I were just happy to hang out with you. Duw, Duw. (*Beat.*) One long road of broken dreams. You get to the end feeling shit and there's the washing to go on. (*Beat.*) We do have some conversations, don't we?

Pause.

JAYNE. I have an impression. Of something. Missing. Something behind my ear. Like a bite. And it won't. Come.

Pause.

It was like being peeled when they told me. I find myself examining shapes. Shifting in clouds. And. I want to wave. In all that colour – something will come together or drift apart and I cannot imagine. That if I don't look hard enough. She won't be there. Just her foot, even. Dangling. Or a wave back. Just to see her and nothing there.

BLODWEN. You are her. You're y'here.

JAYNE. Not even to touch. And this is the legacy of all that life.

Pause.

I feel like I've taken everything they stood for and gone backwards with it. Christ, you just want to leap through oblivion to get to them and it's too fucking late.

BLODWEN. Annoying, that.

JAYNE. I don't know how come I find myself telling you all this, anyway.

BLODWEN. You can put it on a stranger.

Pause.

Do you remember when your dad went?

JAYNE. Vaguely.

BLODWEN. Most beautiful funeral in the history of life, your dad's.

JAYNE. Were you there?

BLODWEN. Awful on you, your mam was nearly tripping over with the weight on it. I remember singing at the top of my strength trying to reach you, sang my heart out for you to feel better.

(*Singing.*) Drop Thy still dews of quietness
'Til all our strivings cease
Take from our souls the strain and stress
And let our ordered lives confess
The beauty of Thy peace
The beauty of Thy peace.

I never took my eyes off you both. I'd never seen no one in black I thought you looked like angels.

JAYNE. Don't.

BLODWEN. I stood at the back. You never broke hands. You looked like one person at the front of that chapel. You cried like you was singing to him, pair on you. Duw, you was broken.

JAYNE. Don't.

BLODWEN. No, you need to know! I felt sick about it. Sick. I couldn't stand it that you was feeling all that love, your family. Sad, like. I felt sorry for it, but the love the three on you had, I couldn't take. I loved you and I hated you in the same moment. Your mam let me stay over that night.

JAYNE. Did she?

BLODWEN. She said, 'Blodwen, this is one of life's many land-marks. Some of them are bloody ugly to look at.' Why you moved away, weren't it? So you no more had to look on ugly.

JAYNE. I remember her telling me not to frown. She said, 'You'll get lines.' I've got lines.

BLODWEN. That's just a map of where you been. I got home the next day right, and my mam pushed me down the stairs for poking my nose in where it weren't wanted.

JAYNE. Did she?

BLODWEN. She did she.

JAYNE. You were wanted.

BLODWEN. And she tore out some of my hair. Must of been hard on her, like. I were never meant to be here, see?

JAYNE. We're all meant to be here.

BLODWEN. I'm not legitimate, am I? So that counts me out.

JAYNE. Oh Christ. Not that.

BLODWEN. Impossible task for her that, round y'here.

JAYNE. Blodwen. You should've come with us.

BLODWEN. I'd be out of my pod up London. She is a cow, mind.

JAYNE. Yes. She is.

BLODWEN. S'alright. I had you for the rescue. You was great. You'd march me up to the top of Tick Hill and make me scream it all out up at God. You always reckoned the sun shone better round the other side of that hill. Then you'd take me back down and poach an egg in vinegar on the wood stove in your yard. You taught me to poach the best egg.

JAYNE. Who, me?

BLODWEN. I always had you on the horizon. So. No. See.

JAYNE. Let's pretend it's all come back to me.

BLODWEN. D'you want to?

JAYNE. Yeah.

BLODWEN. Won't be the first time you saved my great fat arse.

JAYNE. Right then. Jayne.

BLODWEN. That's my name, don't wear it out. Set us an Impossible Task!

JAYNE. Leave your husband.

BLODWEN. That's possible. I just can't be arsed.

JAYNE. Bring Emily up unscarred.

BLODWEN. Look at the state of this fucking linoleum. I'll get buried in the bloody larder. (*Beat*.) Cuts and bruises. She might as well be prepared.

JAYNE. She wants to be an astronaut.

BLODWEN. I know.

JAYNE. Did she tell you?

BLODWEN. No. I were listening at doors. See, why can't she want to work in a shop like every other cow? She has all this to come.

JAYNE. You can't do anything about that.

BLODWEN. Oh and listen to you, fickle as fate! (*Beat*.) I'll buy her some binocliars for her Christmas. (*Beat*.) I wasn't worried if she'd come back, she takes after me. I go up the station. Once a month. Or twice. Just to wait for the train to come in. And I think, where will it take me if I want to go? Just a few moments I spend up the station once a month. Or twice. Thinking about getting away.

JAYNE. I understand that. I understand.

BLODWEN. You always did. I'll never go nowhere, mind. Furniture will see to that. You went. You want to make the most of that.

JAYNE. You knew the train times, then?

BLODWEN. Is that alright?

JAYNE. Bit late now, isn't it?

BLODWEN. Right. Up the wooden hill.

JAYNE. Don't let the bedbugs bite.

BLODWEN. Christ, don't bring that up, they're all over. (*Beat*.) D'you mind if I put her out the door?

JAYNE. No – Who?

BLODWEN. I'll put her out by Rosemary. I'm not crazy for death in the house.

BLODWEN *puts the urn just outside the front door,* JAYNE *watches her. Pause.*

JAYNE. I didn't leave her in the pub. Did I?

BLODWEN. Sorry.

JAYNE. Oh, you mad cow.

BLODWEN. She's in good hands there.

Rosemary bush gone wild. She knocks on the door when the wind comes. I made it up for Em so she's not on her own. (*Beat*.) I'm sorry I said about your urn.

JAYNE. I'm not having sorry, Jayne.

BLODWEN. I'm glad you come back, I were wearing you out.

JAYNE. Did you book me a taxi for the morning?

BLODWEN. You'd forget your bloody head!

Lights.

Scene Three

The next day. EMILY *comes downstairs, goes into the kitchen, the sound of a kettle going on – comes out. Puts the twenty-pound note back in* JAYNE'*s purse, during:*

EMILY (*singing*).
    I wish I were a fascinating bitch
    I'd never be poor, I'd always be rich
    I'd live in a house with a big red light
    I'd sleep all day and I'd work all night
    And every now and then I'd take a holiday
    Just to make my customers wild

JAYNE *comes downstairs, half-dressed in her own clothes.*

    I wish I were a fascinating bitch
    And not an illegitimate child.

I'm doing your tea.

JAYNE. Thank you.

EMILY. Can I do your make-up later?

JAYNE. Er – yeah. If you want.

EMILY. Maybe that's what I'll do instead. I could do make-up for old ladies and they can still face the world.

JAYNE. You cheeky sod. It's got nothing to do with make-up, Em. I wish it bloody did.

EMILY. No, 'cos you've not got a boyfriend, have you?

JAYNE. I have impossibly high standards, actually.

EMILY. My mam's never. Not if it's doing her sister.

EMILY *goes out.* BLODWEN *comes in with* JAYNE's *blouse.*

BLODWEN. Morning, love.

JAYNE. Morning.

BLODWEN. You alright?

JAYNE. Yeah, you?

BLODWEN. No.

BLODWEN *has a pair of knickers poking out of one trouser leg.* JAYNE *gets the giggles.*

I done your clothing. What's the matter, did someone walk on your grave?

JAYNE. No, you've . . .

JAYNE *grabs the knickers.*

BLODWEN. Oh my aching pissflaps. If I'd known I were going to meet you, I'd of gone on a diet. I'm as fat as a wren. Did you sleep?

JAYNE. Like a child. Stand sideways.

BLODWEN. How's that?

JAYNE. Takes pounds off you.

BLODWEN. You are good. You doing tea, Em?

EMILY (*offstage*). Yeah.

BLODWEN. Good girl. Taxi'll be y'here in a minty. D'you want some breakfast?

JAYNE. No, I'm fine thanks.

BLODWEN. 'Cos Em'll do it.

JAYNE. I'm okay.

Pause.

BLODWEN. I won't come with you. Up the station.

JAYNE. No. Don't.

BLODWEN. I don't want to wear it out.

EMILY *comes in with mugs of tea.* BLODWEN *goes into the kitchen.*

JAYNE. What are you doing today, Em?

EMILY. Polishing the clock. I won't tell her. That I know. Does she know?

JAYNE. About – ?

EMILY. Allun.

JAYNE. That you know? Yes.

EMILY. I won't tell her.

BLODWEN *comes in.*

That I know she knows I know.

JAYNE. No – Polishing the clock?

EMILY. Yes.

EMILY *goes out to the kitchen.*

JAYNE. You not working?

BLODWEN. No. I've to go to an auction of promises. Does she know?

JAYNE. About / – Allun?

BLODWEN. About Allun.

JAYNE. That you know that she knows you know? She knows.

BLODWEN. She doesn't need to know I know.

JAYNE. Yeah. No.

EMILY *comes out of the kitchen.*

An auction of promises?

BLODWEN. D'you remember them, do you?

JAYNE. Yes. Yes. I do.

BLODWEN. Remember you're a plum!

JAYNE. Absolutely! I'll try.

EMILY *goes out to the kitchen.*

BLODWEN. Will you take her up the mountain when you go?

EMILY *starts reciting 'Lion Hunt' – 'We came across a mountain, we couldn't go under it, we couldn't go through it, we'll have to go over it . . . '*

JAYNE. Yeah. Yes. I think I will. Before I go.

BLODWEN. You decided?

JAYNE. It's not my landscape to end in, is it? It's not up to me to decide.

BLODWEN. She's gone to a better place.

JAYNE. We haven't been yet! (*Beat.*) Her absence. Will be. A great presence.

BLODWEN. That's it. (*Beat.*) What will you do when you get home?

EMILY (*offstage*). You should make yourself some lovely tea!

JAYNE. Yeah! Maybe I'll poach an egg.

BLODWEN. Listening at doors!

EMILY (*offstage*). D'you hear that, Mam?

BLODWEN. Yes, love. Hefyn the Tall's alarm.

JAYNE gets her things together.

(*Indicating the photograph.*) Don't forget this.

JAYNE. Are you sure?

BLODWEN. No, I'll keep it for the cat. Don't be a pain! It's nice to get a bit of yourself back you've given away.

JAYNE. I won't say goodbye to Em.

BLODWEN. No. You've made your impression.

Beat.

JAYNE. No.

BLODWEN. Oh wait up. I made your tuck.

JAYNE. When did you do that?

BLODWEN. In the night.

BLODWEN goes out to the kitchen. Comes back with a small carrier bag.

JAYNE. Blodwen. (*Beat.*) Thanks. For. Everything.

BLODWEN. Thank you, you old cow. Just enough to be going on with.

I left out your Scotch eggs. Sorry.

The sound of a taxi pulling up. It beeps its horn. JAYNE is overcome by grief.

Come y'here.

JAYNE. You've set me off! Kill you with kindness.

BLODWEN. Kill you with kindness. 'Ladybird ladybird, fly away home.'

JAYNE. I don't even cry normally!

BLODWEN. You do!

JAYNE. Don't start! You sure you don't want me to do Angharad for you?

BLODWEN. No, I'd like to smack up her head, but I won't. Blod?

JAYNE. Yes, Jayne?

BLODWEN. Go flower.

JAYNE. Don't let the bastards grind you down.

BLODWEN. He won't.

> BLODWEN *opens the door, sees the urn.*

Oh Christ! Don't forget to take her with you!

JAYNE. Oh God, no!

BLODWEN. You'll think I done that deliberate so'd you'd never get away!

JAYNE. Bye.

BLODWEN. Hello!

> JAYNE *picks up the urn and leaves.* BLODWEN *finds the photograph* JAYNE'*s forgotten, sits down on the sofa.*
>
> *Silence.*

EMILY (*offstage*). Mam? Mam, can / I have – ?

BLODWEN. No, you cowing can't!

> *Lights.*
>
> *The End.*

A Nick Hern Book

Cariad first published in Great Britain as a paperback original in 2008
by Nick Hern Books Limited, 14 Larden Road, London W3 7ST, in
association with Clwyd Theatr Cymru

Cariad copyright © 2008 Sophie Stanton

Sophie Stanton has asserted her right to be identified as the author of
this work

Cover image: Dewynters
Cover design: Ned Hoste, 2H

Typeset by Nick Hern Books, London
Printed and bound in Great Britain by CPI Antony Rowe

A CIP catalogue record for this book is available from the British
Library

ISBN 978 1 85459 549 2